Nonfiction
Reading
Practice

GRADE **5**

Reading at ❸ Levels

Nonfiction Reading Practice contains 17 units that provide practice with nonfiction reading and comprehension. The unique format is designed to accommodate students' varied reading levels.

Each unit includes:

- a teacher resource page with a suggested teaching path.

- a Visual Literacy page to enrich learning.

- Words to Know lists of reading selection–specific vocabulary.

- text-based questions.

- a writing prompt and Writing Form.

- three reading selections on the same topic. The reading selections progress in difficulty from easiest (Level 1) to hardest (Level 3). The level is shown on the student pages through the use of icons:

  ■ **Level 1**

  ■ ■ **Level 2**

  ■ ■ ■ **Level 3**

Writing: Teera Safi
Keli Winters
Content Editing: Lisa Vitarisi Mathews
Copy Editing: Laurie Westrich
Art Direction: Yuki Meyer
Cover Design: Yuki Meyer
Design/Production: Jessica Onken

EMC 3235

Evan-Moor®
Helping Children Learn

Visit
teaching-standards.com
to view a correlation
of this book.
This is a free service.

**Correlated to
Current Standards**

Congratulations on your purchase of some of the finest teaching materials in the world.

CPSIA: Asia Pacific Offset Ltd, Kowloon, Hong Kong [7/2019]

Contents

What's Inside?

Nonfiction Reading Practice provides 17 units of nonfiction reading selections with topics that span the curriculum. The reading selections progress in difficulty from easiest (Level 1) to hardest (Level 3). Each unit is self-contained and includes materials to provide a rich reading and writing lesson. The contents of each unit is described below.

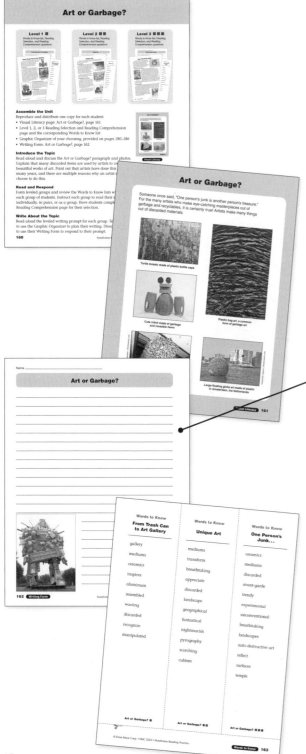

A Teacher Resource Page

A teacher resource page shows unit-specific materials, lists page numbers, and has a suggested teaching path that includes support to introduce the topic.

A Visual Aid

The Visual Literacy page provides information about the topic. This page supports all of the leveled reading selections and is intended to be used as a reference for students in addition to the reading selection.

A Writing Form

The Writing Form is an illustrated page on which students respond to the reading selection–specific writing prompts. The Writing Form in each unit is designed to be used with all three writing prompts.

Vocabulary

The Words to Know lists contain vocabulary for each leveled reading selection. The lists include content vocabulary, phonetically challenging words, and words that may be unfamiliar to students. Words to Know lists must be reproduced and cut apart.

Reading Selections at Three Reading Levels

Each unit presents three reading selections on the same topic. The reading selections progress in difficulty from easiest (Level 1) to hardest (Level 3). An icon indicates the level of the reading selection—Level 1 (■), Level 2 (■ ■), Level 3 (■ ■ ■). Each reading selection contains topic-specific vocabulary and concepts to incorporate into classroom discussion. The Level 1 reading selection gives readers a core vocabulary and a basic understanding of the topic. More challenging vocabulary words are used and additional details are provided as the level of the reading selections increases.

Comprehension Questions

A comprehension page follows each reading selection. There are text-dependent questions in multiple-choice and constructed response formats. The open-ended questions are intended to elicit higher-order thinking skills. As a result, answers will vary.

A Writing Prompt

Write About the Topic, a text-based writing prompt, is given at the bottom of each comprehension page. Students use the Writing Form to write their response. If you plan to display students' writing on a bulletin board, you may wish to have students complete a rough draft on another piece of paper.

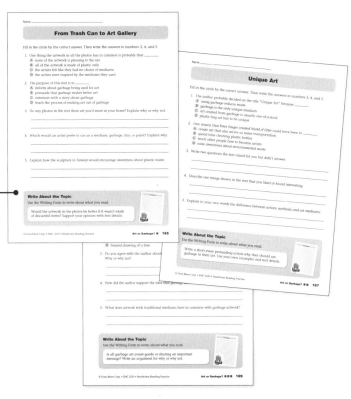

Graphic Organizers

There are seven graphic organizers to help students plan their writing and extend comprehension. The graphic organizers are located on pages 180–186 at the back of the book.

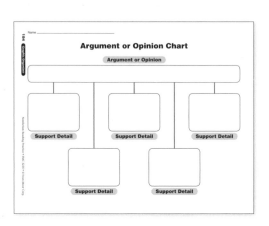

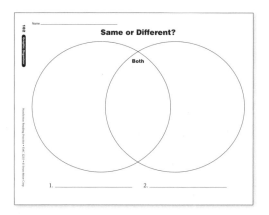

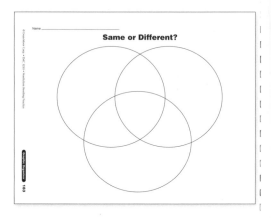

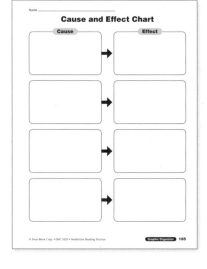

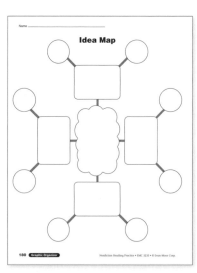

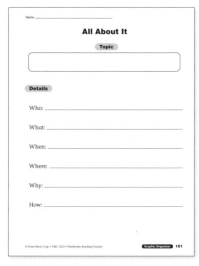

More About *Nonfiction Reading Practice*

Reading Nonfiction Is Important

Research indicates that students are not reading enough nonfiction texts. One reason reading nonfiction is so important is that it helps students develop background knowledge, which accounts for as much as 33 percent of the variance in student achievement (Marzano, 2000). Background knowledge becomes more crucial in the later elementary grades as students begin to read more content-specific textbooks (Young, Moss, & Cornwell, 2007), which often include headings, graphs, charts, and other text elements not often found in the narrative fiction they encountered in the lower grades (Sanacore & Palumbo, 2009).

Readability

All of the reading selections in this series have been edited for readability. Readability formulas, which are mathematical calculations, are considered to be one way of predicting reading ease. The Lexile® Analyzer was used to check for readability. The Lexile® Analyzer measures the complexity of the text by studying its characteristics, such as sentence length, word difficulty, and word frequency. We have used the new Lexile® grade-level spans, as recommended in the Common Core State Standards, to determine where each Lexile® score falls within a grade level.

Planning Instruction

The units in this book do not need to be taught in sequential order. Choose the units that align with your curriculum or with student interests.

- For whole-group instruction, introduce the unit to the whole class. Provide each student with a reading selection at the appropriate reading level. Guide students as they read the reading selections. You may want to have students read with partners. Then conduct a class discussion to share the different information learned.

- For small-group instruction, choose a reading selection at the appropriate reading level for each group. The group reads the reading selection with teacher guidance and discusses the information presented.

- The reading selections may also be used to assist readers in moving from less difficult to more challenging reading material. After building vocabulary and familiarity with the topic at the appropriate level, students may be able to successfully read the reading selection at the next level of difficulty.

Name: _____

Reading Checklist

Before I Read

☐ I think about what I already know.

☐ I think about what I want to learn.

☐ I read the title for clues.

☐ I look at the pictures for clues.

While I Read

☐ I stop and identify the main idea.

☐ I underline important details.

☐ I read the captions below the pictures.

☐ I make pictures of the text in my mind.

☐ I write down questions I have.

☐ I use words I understand to help me figure out words I don't know.

After I Read

☐ I think about the author's purpose.

☐ I speak, draw, and write about what I read.

☐ I reread my favorite parts.

☐ I reread to find details.

☐ I look back at the text to find the answers to questions.

☐ I think about the information I've learned in order to answer questions.

Name: _____

My Reading and Writing Record

Write the title of the reading selection you read. Then make a checkmark in the box if you completed the other tasks. Write **yes** or **no** to tell if you liked the topic.

I read...	I answered questions	I planned my writing	I wrote	I liked this topic

The Iroquois Nations

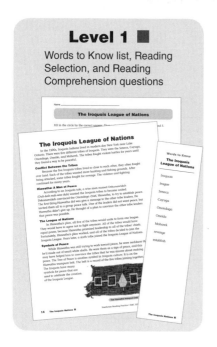

Level 1 ■
Words to Know list, Reading Selection, and Reading Comprehension questions

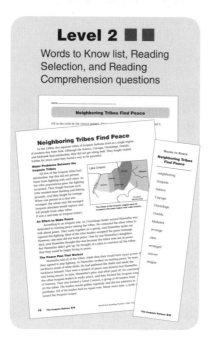

Level 2 ■ ■
Words to Know list, Reading Selection, and Reading Comprehension questions

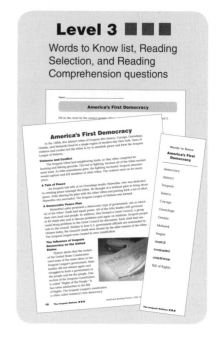

Level 3 ■ ■ ■
Words to Know list, Reading Selection, and Reading Comprehension questions

Assemble the Unit

Reproduce and distribute one copy for each student:

- Visual Literacy page: The Iroquois Nations, 1600s, page 11
- Level 1, 2, or 3 Reading Selection and Reading Comprehension page and the corresponding Words to Know list
- Graphic Organizer of your choosing, provided on pages 180–186
- Writing Form: The Iroquois Nations, page 12

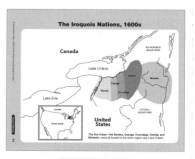

Visual Literacy

Introduce the Topic

Read aloud and discuss The Iroquois Nations, 1600s map. Explain that the five Iroquois tribes lived in the same region near Lake Ontario in what is now New York State, and they fought for many years. Tell students that it is believed by some that the Iroquois League of Nations was formed between the years 1570 and 1600.

Read and Respond

Form leveled groups and review the Words to Know lists with each group of students. Instruct each group to read their selection individually, in pairs, or as a group. Have students complete the Reading Comprehension page for their selection.

Writing Form

Write About the Topic

Read aloud the leveled writing prompt for each group. Tell students to use the Graphic Organizer to plan their writing. Direct students to use their Writing Form to respond to their prompt.

The Iroquois Nations, 1600s

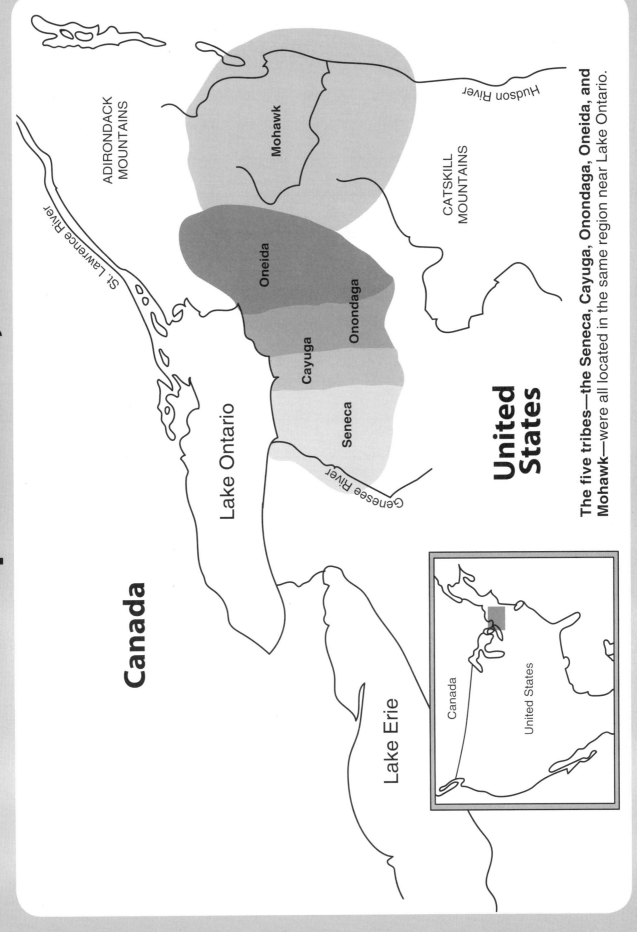

ADIRONDACK MOUNTAINS

Mohawk

Hudson River

CATSKILL MOUNTAINS

St. Lawrence River

Oneida

Cayuga

Onondaga

Seneca

Genesee River

Lake Ontario

Canada

Lake Erie

United States

The five tribes—the **Seneca, Cayuga, Onondaga, Oneida,** and **Mohawk**—were all located in the same region near Lake Ontario.

Canada

United States

Name _____

The Iroquois Nations

_____

_____

_____

_____

_____

_____

_____

_____

_____

_____

_____

_____

_____

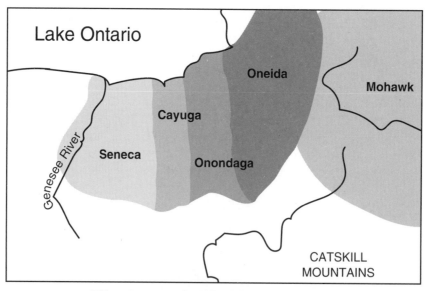

The Iroquois Nations, 1600s

Words to Know	Words to Know	Words to Know
The Iroquois League of Nations	**Neighboring Tribes Find Peace**	**America's First Democracy**
Iroquois	neighboring	democracy
league	Iroquois	distinct
Seneca	Seneca	Iroquois
Cayuga	Cayuga	Seneca
Onondaga	Onondaga	Cayuga
Oneida	Oneida	Onondaga
Mohawk	Mohawk	Oneida
revenge	revenge	Mohawk
establish	clan	league
	wronged	council
	sincere	nominated
	league	constitution
		Bill of Rights
The Iroquois Nations ■	The Iroquois Nations ■ ■	The Iroquois Nations ■ ■ ■

The Iroquois League of Nations

In the 1500s, Iroquois Indians lived in modern-day New York near Lake Ontario. There were five different tribes of Iroquois. They were the Seneca, Cayuga, Onondaga, Oneida, and Mohawk. The tribes fought violent battles for years until they found a way to be peaceful.

Conflict Between the Tribes

Because the five Iroquois tribes lived so close to each other, they often fought over land. Each of the tribes wanted more hunting and fishing grounds. After being attacked, some tribes fought for revenge. The violence and fighting continued for many years.

Hiawatha: A Man of Peace

According to an Iroquois tale, a wise man named Dekanawidah (Duh-kah-nuh-wee-duh) wanted the Iroquois tribes to become united. Dekanawidah convinced the Onondaga chief, Hiawatha, to try to establish peace. The first thing Hiawatha did was give a message to the other tribe leaders. He invited them all to a group peace talk. One of the leaders did not want peace, but Hiawatha didn't give up. He thought of a plan to convince the other tribe leaders that peace was possible.

The League of Nations

In Hiawatha's plan, all five of the tribes would unite to form one league. They would have to agree not to fight anymore. All of the tribes would have equal power, because Hiawatha promised leadership to all of the tribes' chiefs. Fortunately, Hiawatha's plan worked, and all of the tribes decided to join the Iroquois League. Years later, a sixth tribe joined the Iroquois League of Nations.

Symbols of Peace

While Hiawatha was still trying to work toward peace, he wore necklaces that he'd made out of small white shells. He wore them as a sign of peace, and this may have helped him to convince the tribes that he was sincere about making peace. The Tree of Peace is another symbol in Iroquois culture. It is on the Hiawatha wampum belt. The belt is a record of the five tribes joining together.

The Iroquois have many symbols for peace that are used to celebrate the creation of the Iroquois League.

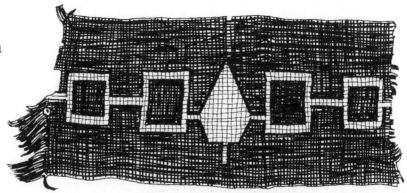

The Hiawatha wampum belt

Nonfiction Reading Practice • EMC 3235 • © Evan-Moor Corp.

The Iroquois League of Nations

Fill in the circle by the correct answer. Then write the answers to numbers 3, 4, and 5.

1. In this text, "league" probably means a _____.
   Ⓐ peaceful individual
   Ⓑ unified group
   Ⓒ tribe
   Ⓓ geographical area

2. What is the relationship between the tribes' geographical locations and the fighting?
   Ⓐ They experienced similar climates and weather.
   Ⓑ Being so far apart made them fear each other more.
   Ⓒ The tribes shared the same ancestors.
   Ⓓ Being so close made them compete for land.

3. Is there any justification for why one chief did not want peace? Explain your answer.

   _____

   _____

4. In your opinion, why did all the tribes eventually agree to be peaceful?

   _____

   _____

5. Explain how the Hiawatha wampum belt is related to peace.

   _____

   _____

Write About the Topic

Use the Writing Form to write about what you read.

How would you support the conclusion that without Hiawatha, the tribes would not have had peace? Use details from the text.

Neighboring Tribes Find Peace

In the 1500s, five separate tribes of Iroquois Indians lived in a single region of modern-day New York. Although the Seneca, Cayuga, Onondaga, Oneida, and Mohawk had similarities, they did not get along well. They fought violent battles for years until they found a way to be peaceful.

Major Problems Between the Iroquois Tribes

All five of the Iroquois tribes had similarities, but this did not prevent them from fighting with each other. As the tribe populations grew, the fighting increased. They fought because each tribe wanted more hunting and fishing grounds, and they fought for revenge. When one person in a clan was wronged, the whole clan felt wronged. Iroquois attackers would capture and kill people from other tribes. It was a sad time in Iroquois history.

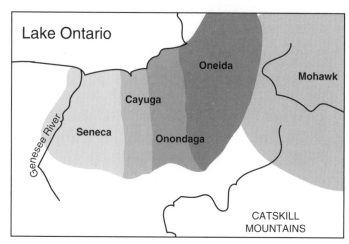

The tribes of the Iroquois League were all located in the same region near Lake Ontario.

An Effort to Make Peace

According to an Iroquois tale, an Onondaga leader named Hiawatha was dedicated to creating peace among the tribes. He contacted the other tribes to talk about peace. They came together as a group, and Hiawatha spoke out against the fighting. Most of the tribe leaders accepted the peace message. However, one man did not want peace. One by one Hiawatha's daughters died, and Hiawatha thought this was because the tribes were not at peace. But Hiawatha didn't give up. He thought of a plan to convince all the tribes that they could be happy living in peace.

The Peace Plan That Worked

Hiawatha told all of the tribes' chiefs that they would have equal power if they agreed to stop fighting. As Hiawatha worked on making peace, he wore necklaces made of white shells. He had gathered the shells and made the necklaces himself. They were a symbol of peace and showed that Hiawatha was being sincere. In time, Hiawatha's plan and effort paid off. He convinced the other Iroquois leaders to make peace, and they formed the Iroquois League of Nations. They also formed a Great Council, a group of 49 leaders from all the tribes. The leaders would gather regularly and discuss solutions to problems. All of the leaders had an equal vote. Many years later, a sixth tribe joined the Iroquois League.

Name _____

Neighboring Tribes Find Peace

Fill in the circle by the correct answer. Then write the answers to numbers 3, 4, and 5.

1. The map shows that the five tribes _____.
   Ⓐ all had equal amounts of land
   Ⓑ were separated by Lake Ontario
   Ⓒ lived close to each other
   Ⓓ were basically one single tribe

2. Which of these was the main cause of fighting between the Iroquois tribes?
   Ⓐ Each tribe wanted more hunting and fishing grounds.
   Ⓑ Each tribe wanted a larger population.
   Ⓒ Each tribe wanted more ground to build their homes.
   Ⓓ Each tribe's population decreased.

3. Do you think the population growth justified the fighting among tribes? Explain.

   _____

   _____

4. Would you have agreed to Hiawatha's plan if you were a wronged tribe leader? Explain.

   _____

   _____

5. Why was it better that the Great Council had leaders from all the tribes instead of one?

   _____

   _____

Write About the Topic

Use the Writing Form to write about what you read.

> Explain how Hiawatha's words and actions achieved peace for the Iroquois tribes. Use details from the text in your response.

America's First Democracy

In the 1500s, five distinct tribes of Iroquois (the Seneca, Cayuga, Onondaga, Oneida, and Mohawk) lived in a single region of modern-day New York. Years of violence and conflict led the tribes to try to establish peace and form the Iroquois League of Nations.

Violence and Conflict

The Iroquois tribes had neighboring lands, so they often competed for hunting and fishing grounds. This led to fighting, because all of the tribes wanted more land. As tribe populations grew, the fighting increased. Iroquois attackers would capture and kill members of other tribes. The violence went on for many years.

A Tale of Peace

An Iroquois tale tells of an Onondaga leader, Hiawatha, who was dedicated to creating peace amongst the tribes. He thought of a brilliant plan to bring about peace. After sharing his plan with the other tribes and putting forth a lot of effort, Hiawatha was successful. The Iroquois League of Nations was formed.

A Democratic Peace Plan

Hiawatha's plan promised a democratic type of government, one in which all of the tribes' chiefs had equal power. All of the tribe leaders still governed their own land and people. In addition, they formed a Great Council, a group of 49 chiefs who met to discuss problems and agree on solutions. Iroquois people could bring problems to the Great Council for discussion. Each chief had one vote in the council. Similar to how U.S. government officials are nominated by citizens today, the council's chiefs were chosen by the elder women of the tribes. The Iroquois League even created its own constitution.

The Influence of Iroquois Democracy on the United States

History shows that the writers of the United States Constitution used some of the same ideas as the Iroquois League's government. State leaders did not always agree and struggled to form a government of the people and for the people. One section of the Iroquois Constitution is called "Rights of the People." It has some similarities to the Bill of Rights. The Iroquois League's constitution is often called America's first democracy.

America's First Democracy

Fill in the circle by the correct answer. Then write the answers to numbers 3, 4, and 5.

1. How did the tribes' geographical closeness play a role in their fighting?
   - Ⓐ They had to compete for hunting and fishing grounds.
   - Ⓑ They were confused about who belonged to which tribe.
   - Ⓒ The tribes could easily avoid each other if they wanted to.
   - Ⓓ Tribe leaders were unaware that other tribes existed.

2. What detail made Hiawatha's plan for peace successful?
   - Ⓐ Elder women would make up the Great Council.
   - Ⓑ The Iroquois would be known as the "League of Nations."
   - Ⓒ All of the tribe leaders had equal power.
   - Ⓓ There would be more hunting and fishing grounds.

3. How did tribe members who weren't chiefs contribute to the Great Council?

   _____

   _____

4. How does the author support the fact that the Iroquois government was democratic?

   _____

   _____

5. Why would the U.S. Constitution's writers use ideas from the Iroquois constitution?

   _____

   _____

Write About the Topic

Use the Writing Form to write about what you read.

Explain why the Iroquois government is known to some people as America's first democracy. Use details from the text.

Women in the American Revolution

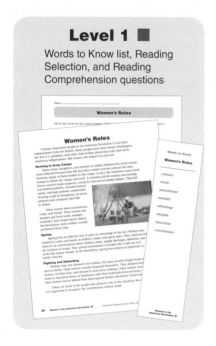
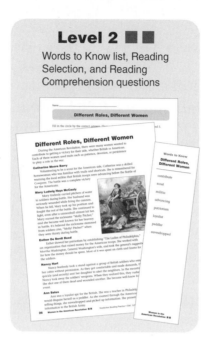
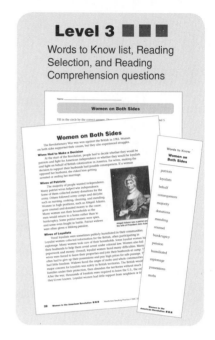
Assemble the Unit

Reproduce and distribute one copy for each student:

- Visual Literacy page: Women in the American Revolution, page 21
- Level 1, 2, or 3 Reading Selection and Reading Comprehension page and the corresponding Words to Know list
- Graphic Organizer of your choosing, provided on pages 180–186
- Writing Form: Women in the American Revolution, page 22

Visual Literacy

Introduce the Topic

Read aloud and discuss the Women in the American Revolution text, portraits, and photographs. Tell students that the photo of the woman mending was taken at a Revolutionary War reenactment. Explain that there were many ways that women contributed to the war.

Read and Respond

Form leveled groups and review the Words to Know lists with each group of students. Instruct each group to read their selection individually, in pairs, or as a group. Have students complete the Reading Comprehension page for their selection.

Writing Form

Write About the Topic

Read aloud the leveled writing prompt for each group. Tell students to use the Graphic Organizer to plan their writing. Direct students to use their Writing Form to respond to their prompt.

Women in the American Revolution

The legend of Molly Pitcher is based on an actual woman who took her husband's place in battle and bravely fought until the end.

Martha Washington, the country's "first" first lady, raised a huge sum of money to donate to the American troops. She also donated a large sum herself.

Ken Schulze / Shutterstock.com

Many women followed the army camps and did jobs that supported the soldiers. One important job was mending soldiers' clothing.

Abigail Adams gave her husband wise counsel during the Revolution. She ran her family's household and raised the children while her husband worked towards independence.

Name _____

Women in the American Revolution

_____

_____

_____

_____

_____

_____

_____

_____

_____

_____

_____

_____

_____

_____

_____

_____

_____

_____

_____

Nonfiction Reading Practice • EMC 3235 • © Evan-Moor Corp.

Words to Know	Words to Know	Words to Know
Women's Roles	**Different Roles, Different Women**	**Women on Both Sides**
colonial	contribute	patriots
wards	scout	loyalists
seamstresses	militia	behalf
mended	advancing	consequences
advantage	patriotism	majority
adopted	loyalist	donations
masculine	peddler	mending
contributions	eavesdropped	counsel
		bankruptcy
		pension
		humiliated
		espionage
		possessions
		mobs

Women in the American Revolution ■	**Women in the American Revolution** ■ ■	**Women in the American Revolution** ■ ■ ■

© Evan-Moor Corp. • EMC 3235 • Nonfiction Reading Practice

Words to Know 23

Women's Roles

Colonial Americans fought in the American Revolution to win their independence from the British. Many people know that George Washington, the first U.S. president, and other male leaders played key roles that led to American independence. But women also helped win the war.

Working in Army Camps

Many wives, daughters, and mothers of soldiers followed the army camps. Some followed because they felt that they couldn't survive without the men. However, many of them worked in the camps. In fact, the American army hired women to follow the camps and work. A common job for women was nursing. Nurses assisted male surgeons, caring for sick and wounded soldiers. They fed and bathed patients, cleaned medical wards, and kept patients comfortable. Nursing could be dangerous, as many patients and caregivers died due to illness.

Other women were seamstresses, cooks, and maids. These women did laundry, got fresh water, mended uniforms, and cooked meals. Before the Revolution, male soldiers usually performed these roles.

Spying

Spying was an effective way to gain an advantage in the war. Women who worked as cooks and maids in military camps were great spies. They could secretly listen in on conversations about military plans, supply shortages, deliveries, and the location of troops. They passed information to people who could use it to make the enemy weaker. In the Revolution, spying was almost as important as battle victories.

Fighting and Defending

Women were not allowed to be soldiers, but some secretly fought beside the men in battle. These women usually disguised themselves. They adopted male names, cut their hair, and dressed in masculine clothing. Other women stayed at home to maintain farms or businesses until their husbands returned home. Often, these women had to defend their land against British and Native American troops.

When we think of the people who played a role in the American Revolution, it is important to recognize the contributions women made.

Women's Roles

Fill in the circle by the correct answer. Then write the answers to numbers 3, 4, and 5.

1. The women who followed the army camps but didn't work probably _____.
   Ⓐ were a burden on the soldiers' resources
   Ⓑ were pleased to leave their homes
   Ⓒ became spies after a few years
   Ⓓ had an interest in watching the battles

2. The American army probably hired women to do camp jobs _____.
   Ⓐ because otherwise the women would be alone at home
   Ⓑ so that male soldiers could focus on the war
   Ⓒ so the women would get to see what battle looks like
   Ⓓ because it was impossible for male soldiers to do the jobs

3. Why do you think the nurses were so important to the war effort?

   _____

   _____

4. Why do you think spying was almost as important as battle victories?

   _____

   _____

5. How does the author support the fact that women fought and defended during the war?

   _____

   _____

Write About the Topic

Use the Writing Form to write about what you read.

Explain how women affected the outcome of the American Revolution. Use details from the text in your response.

Different Roles, Different Women

During the American Revolution, there were many women who wanted to contribute to getting a victory for their side, whether British or American. Each of these women used traits such as patience, devotion, or persistence to play a role in the war.

Catherine Moore Barry

Volunteering to be a scout for the American side, Catherine was a skilled horsewoman who was familiar with trails and shortcuts. She is remembered for warning the local militia that British troops were advancing before the Battle of Cowpens. The battle was a complete victory for the Americans.

Mary Ludwig Hays McCauly

Mary tirelessly carried pitchers of water to soldiers during battle. Her husband was seriously wounded while firing the cannon. When he fell, Mary took up his position and fought the rest of the battle. She continued to fight, even after a cannonball almost hit her. Mary earned the nickname "Molly Pitcher," and she became well known for her bravery in battle. It's believed the nickname stemmed from soldiers' cries, "Molly! Pitcher!" when they were thirsty during battle.

Esther De Berdt Reed

Esther showed her patriotism by establishing "The Ladies of Philadelphia," an organization that raised money for the American troops. She worked with Martha Washington, General Washington's wife, and took the general's suggestion for how the money should be spent. Most of it was spent on cloth and linens for the soldiers.

Nancy Hart

Nancy fearlessly took a stand against a group of British soldiers who entered her cabin without permission. As they got comfortable and made demands, Hart quickly (and secretly) sent her daughter to alert the neighbors. In the meantime, Nancy took away the soldiers' weapons. When they realized this, they rushed her. She shot one of them dead and wounded another. She became well known for this event.

Ann Bates

Ann was a loyalist spy for the British. She was a teacher in Philadelphia, but would disguise herself as a peddler. As she roamed through the American camps selling things, she eavesdropped and picked up information. She passed the information to the British Army.

Different Roles, Different Women

Fill in the circle by the correct answer. Then write the answers to numbers 3, 4, and 5.

1. Nancy Hart's actions could be categorized as _____.
   - Ⓐ spying on the enemy
   - Ⓑ fighting in battle
   - Ⓒ defending herself and her land
   - Ⓓ influencing others

2. Most of the women in the text were _____.
   - Ⓐ British loyalists
   - Ⓑ influential writers
   - Ⓒ in organizations
   - Ⓓ American patriots

3. Which of the women would you interview and why?

   _____

   _____

4. What actions did Mary demonstrate that would cause you to think she was brave?

   _____

   _____

5. What was Ann Bates's motive for acting the way she did during the war?

   _____

   _____

Write About the Topic

Use the Writing Form to write about what you read.

> What traits can you infer about the women from their roles in the war? Compare three of them using details from the text.

Women on Both Sides

The Revolutionary War was won against the British in 1783. Women on both sides supported their causes, but they also experienced struggles.

Wives Had to Make a Decision

At the start of the Revolution, people had to decide whether they would be patriots and fight for American independence or whether they would be loyalists and fight on behalf of British colonization in America. For wives, making the decision to support their husbands had possible consequences. If a woman opposed her husband, she risked him getting arrested or ending her marriage.

Wives of Patriots

The majority of people wanted independence. Many patriot wives helped win independence. Some of them collected money donations for the army. Others followed army camps and did jobs such as nursing, cooking, cleaning, and mending. Women in high positions, such as Abigail Adams, gave counsel and donated money to the cause. Many women ran their households so the men would return to a home rather than to bankruptcy. Some patriot women were spies, and some even fought in battle. Patriot widows were often given a lifelong pension.

Abigail Adams was a patriot and the wife of President John Adams.

Wives of Loyalists

Vocal loyalists were sometimes publicly humiliated in their communities. Loyalist women collected information for the British, often participating in espionage. Many women took care of their households. Some loyalist women hid their husbands to help them avoid arrest under colonial law. Women also hid paperwork and money. Overall, loyalist women faced many difficulties. Many wives were forced to leave their properties and join their husbands at camp. They often had to give up their possessions and pay high prices for safe passage. They had little freedom. Widows faced the anger of mobs and whole communities. A major concern for loyalists was safety in British territories. The British would invite families under their protection, then abandon the territories without much notice. After the war, thousands of loyalists were required to leave the U.S., the only home they'd ever known. Loyalist women had little support from neighbors or friends.

Name _____

Women on Both Sides

Fill in the circle by the correct answer. Then write the answers to numbers 3, 4, and 5.

1. Many loyalist wives _____.
   - Ⓐ lost their husbands and their properties
   - Ⓑ were given lifelong pensions
   - Ⓒ supported the patriots
   - Ⓓ gave information to the patriots

2. Why would a woman decide to be a loyalist?
   - Ⓐ She believed that America should form its own country.
   - Ⓑ She wanted to leave her property and her home.
   - Ⓒ She was heavily influenced by Abigail Adams.
   - Ⓓ She believed that America should remain colonized.

3. How could a wife justify her decision to be a patriot or a loyalist in the Revolution?

   _____

   _____

4. Describe why the British territories were or were not safe for loyalists.

   _____

   _____

5. How would the outcome have been different for loyalists if the British had won the war?

   _____

   _____

Write About the Topic

Use the Writing Form to write about what you read.

Compare and contrast the concerns, struggles, and roles of patriot and loyalist women. Use details from the text.

Art Reflects History

Level 1 ■
Words to Know list, Reading Selection, and Reading Comprehension questions

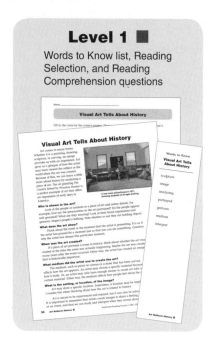

Level 2 ■ ■
Words to Know list, Reading Selection, and Reading Comprehension questions

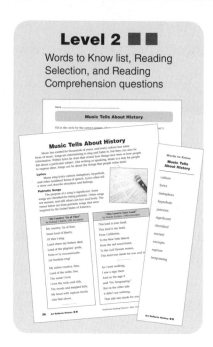

Level 3 ■ ■ ■
Words to Know list, Reading Selection, and Reading Comprehension questions

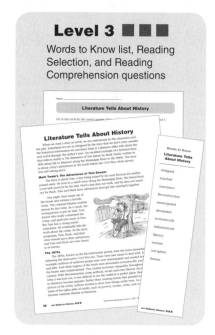

Assemble the Unit

Reproduce and distribute one copy for each student:

- Visual Literacy page: Art Reflects History Timeline, page 31
- Level 1, 2, or 3 Reading Selection and Reading Comprehension page and the corresponding Words to Know list
- Graphic Organizer of your choosing, provided on pages 180–186
- Writing Form: Art Reflects History, page 32

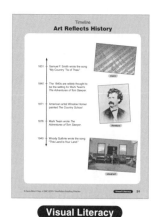

Visual Literacy

Introduce the Topic

Read aloud and discuss the Art Reflects History Timeline. Explain that visual art, music, and literature reflect how the artist, musician, or author saw history or chose to portray it. Explain that art that portrays history was not necessarily created during the time period it is addressing.

Read and Respond

Form leveled groups and review the Words to Know lists with each group of students. Instruct each group to read their selection individually, in pairs, or as a group. Have students complete the Reading Comprehension page for their selection.

Writing Form

Write About the Topic

Read aloud the leveled writing prompt for each group. Tell students to use the Graphic Organizer to plan their writing. Direct students to use their Writing Form to respond to their prompt.

Nonfiction Reading Practice • EMC 3235 • © Evan-Moor Corp.

Art Reflects History

1831 — Samuel F. Smith wrote the song "My Country 'Tis of Thee."

music

1840 — The 1840s are widely thought to be the setting for Mark Twain's *The Adventures of Tom Sawyer*.

1871 — American artist Winslow Homer painted *The Country School*

literature

1876 — Mark Twain wrote *The Adventures of Tom Sawyer*.

1940 — Woody Guthrie wrote the song "This Land Is Your Land."

visual art

Name _____

_____

_____

_____

_____

_____

_____

_____

_____

_____

_____

_____

_____

_____

_____

_____

_____

_____

_____

_____

_____

Words to Know

Visual Art Tells About History

sculpture

image

analyzing

portrayed

gestures

medium

interpret

Words to Know

Music Tells About History

culture

lyrics

metaphors

hyperbole

patriotic

significant

cherished

earnest

excerpts

rapture

trespassing

Words to Know

Literature Tells About History

intrigued

mischief

conscience

Reconstruction

emancipated

devastated

economically

industrialized

literary

realism

corruption

themes

Art Reflects History ■

Art Reflects History ■ ■

Art Reflects History ■ ■ ■

Visual Art Tells About History

Art comes in many forms. Whether it is a painting, drawing, sculpture, or carving, an image provides us with an experience. Art gives us a glimpse of how the artist may have viewed the subject or the world when the art was created. Because of this, we can learn a little more about history by analyzing a piece of art. The oil painting *The Country School* by Winslow Homer is a perfect example of art that offers an impression of early days in America.

A one-room schoolhouse in 1871, showing students of all ages working

Who is shown in the art?

Look at the people or animals in a piece of art and notice details. For example, how are the personalities in the art portrayed? Do the people appear well groomed? What are they wearing? Look at their facial expressions and gestures. Inspect people's clothing. Note whether or not they are holding objects.

What does the art show?

Think about the event or the moment that the artist is presenting. It is as if the artist has paused for a moment just so that you can see something. Question why the artist has chosen this particular moment.

When was the art created?

If a piece of art portrays a scene in history, think about whether the art was created at the time the scene was actually happening. Maybe the art was created many years after the event occurred. Either way, the artist has created an image that is historically important.

What medium did the artist use to create the art?

The medium, such as paint on canvas or a stone that has been carved, affects how the art appears. An artist may choose a specific material because of how it looks. Or, an artist may only have enough money to create art with a certain material. Either way, the medium affects how people feel about the art.

What is the setting, or location, of the image?

Art may show a specific location. Sometimes, a location may be implied. Consider this when thinking about how the art is related to history.

Art is meant to be experienced and enjoyed, but it can also be informative. It is important to remember that artists create images to share a feeling, an idea, or an event, and that we can study and interpret what they reveal about history.

Visual Art Tells About History

Fill in the circle by the correct answer. Then write the answers to numbers 3, 4, and 5.

1. How could the bold-text questions in the text be described?
   - Ⓐ questions to answer in order to be an artist
   - Ⓑ guiding questions that help you better understand a piece of art
   - Ⓒ questions that can be asked and answered only about carvings
   - Ⓓ questions that apply only to the painting in the selection

2. How are the people in the painting portrayed?
   - Ⓐ They are in conflict with each other.
   - Ⓑ They are getting ready to go somewhere.
   - Ⓒ They are playing and talking.
   - Ⓓ They busy doing their schoolwork.

3. Write one observation about the people in the painting.

   _____

4. How could you change the painting to portray the people differently?

   _____

   _____

5. Why would the artist choose to paint this moment in history?

   _____

   _____

Write About the Topic

Use the Writing Form to write about what you read.

What does the art show about life during the 1870s in America?
Use details from the text in your response.

Music Tells About History

Music has existed for thousands of years, and every culture has some form of music. Songs are entertaining to sing and listen to, but they can also be informative. Within lyrics lie clues that reveal how things once were or how people felt about a particular subject. Like writing or speaking, music is a way for people to express ideas. Songs can be about the things that people value most.

Lyrics

Many song lyrics contain metaphors, hyperbole, and other nonliteral forms of speech. Lyrics often tell a story and describe situations and feelings.

Patriotic Songs

The purpose of a song is significant. Some songs are cherished for being patriotic. Other songs are earnest, and still others are fun and lively. The verses below are from patriotic songs that were inspired by the United States of America.

"My Country 'Tis of Thee" by Samuel F. Smith, 1831 (excerpts)	**"This Land Is Your Land"** by Woody Guthrie, 1940 (excerpts)
My country, 'tis of thee, Sweet land of liberty, Of thee I sing; Land where my fathers died, Land of the pilgrims' pride, From ev'ry mountainside Let freedom ring! My native country, thee, Land of the noble, free, Thy name I love; I love thy rocks and rills, Thy woods and templed hills, My heart with rapture thrills Like that above.	This land is your land, This land is my land, From California, To the New York Island; From the red wood forest, To the Gulf Stream waters, This land was made for you and me. ——— As I went walking, I saw a sign there And on the sign it said "No Trespassing." But on the other side it didn't say nothing, That side was made for you and me.

   Nonfiction Reading Practice • EMC 3235 • © Evan-Moor Corp.

Name _____

Music Tells About History

Fill in the circle by the correct answer. Then write the answers to numbers 3, 4, and 5.

1. Why does the singer mention pilgrims in "My Country 'Tis of Thee"?
   Ⓐ The song is about how the pilgrims came to America.
   Ⓑ The song is about the area where the pilgrims lived.
   Ⓒ The pilgrims played an important role in America's history.
   Ⓓ Samuel F. Smith was a pilgrim.

2. "This Land Is Your Land" mentions specific places in the U.S. to _____.
   Ⓐ show that the entire country is free, from coast to coast
   Ⓑ provide geographical information in the song
   Ⓒ inform listeners of how far he has traveled
   Ⓓ make the song appeal to people in different areas

3. In Guthrie's song, why does the singer claim that the "other" side is for you and me?

   _____

   _____

4. What details do the songs give us about the geography of the United States of America? Are these details an important part of the songs?

   _____

   _____

5. What things do Americans probably value most, according to these songs?

   _____

   _____

Write About the Topic

Use the Writing Form to write about what you read.

> Compare and contrast the themes in the two songs.
> Use examples from the text to support your statements.

Literature Tells About History

When we read a story or novel, we are entertained by the characters and the plot. Sometimes we are so intrigued by the story that we don't even consider the historical information we can learn from it. Literature often tells about the real world through the author's eyes. An excellent example of a fictional story that reflects reality is *The Adventures of Tom Sawyer* by Mark Twain, written in 1876 about life in Missouri along the Mississippi River in the 1840s. The story is about a boy's adventures in the South before the Civil War, while slavery was still taking place.

Mark Twain's *The Adventures of Tom Sawyer*

The story is about Tom, a boy being raised by his aunt because his mother passed away. He lives in a small town along the Mississippi River. His friend Huck is not well cared for by his dad. Huck's dad does not work, and he does not watch out for Huck. Tom and Huck have adventures (and get into mischief) together.

One night, they sneak out of the house and witness a horrific crime. The criminal blames another person for his crime. As a result, the wrong person is put on trial. Tom knows who really committed the crime, and guilt eats away at him. But Tom has a strong moral conscience. He eventually tells the truth about the crime. As the story progresses, Tom, Huck, and their other friends have other adventures, and Tom and Huck are even found to be heroes.

The 1870s

The 1870s, known as the Reconstruction period, were the years immediately following the destructive Civil War era. There were new issues to deal with. For example, millions of enslaved people were now emancipated and needed homes and jobs. And while regions of the South were devastated economically, parts of the North were industrialized. This created economic inequality throughout the country. With Reconstruction came political, social, and even literary changes. After a war-torn era, it was difficult to see the world as a perfect place. Realism in literature became popular. Rather than creating stories that painted an ideal picture of the world, authors wanted to show how things really were. As a result, some of the uglier sides of reality, such as poverty, racism, crime, and corruption, became common themes in literature.

Literature Tells About History

Fill in the circle by the correct answer. Then write the answers to numbers 3, 4, and 5.

1. What inference can you make about Mark Twain as an author?
   - Ⓐ He is against slavery.
   - Ⓑ He wishes he were a boy again.
   - Ⓒ He felt it was important to write about criminals.
   - Ⓓ He felt it was important to write about life in the South during slavery.

2. *The Adventures of Tom Sawyer* reflects reality by focusing on _____.
   - Ⓐ an American family's ideal life
   - Ⓑ hardship and moral struggles
   - Ⓒ the life of emancipated people
   - Ⓓ the Reconstruction period

3. In your own words, explain what realism is in literature.

   _____

   _____

4. How does the text support the idea that the Civil War caused new issues in the country?

   _____

   _____

5. Would you recommend a fictional book from the 1870s to someone who wants to learn more about American history? Explain why or why not.

   _____

   _____

Write About the Topic

Use the Writing Form to write about what you read.

Describe the relationship between realism, the Reconstruction period, and *The Adventures of Tom Sawyer*. Use examples.

Ways to Earn a Living

Level 1 ■
Words to Know list, Reading Selection, and Reading Comprehension questions

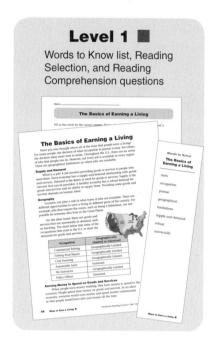

Level 2 ■ ■
Words to Know list, Reading Selection, and Reading Comprehension questions

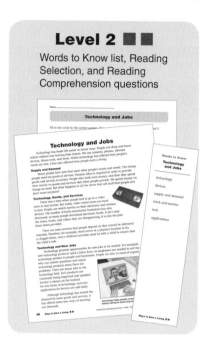

Level 3 ■ ■ ■
Words to Know list, Reading Selection, and Reading Comprehension questions

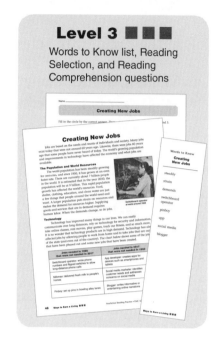

Assemble the Unit

Reproduce and distribute one copy for each student:

- Visual Literacy page: Ways to Earn a Living, page 41
- Level 1, 2, or 3 Reading Selection and Reading Comprehension page and the corresponding Words to Know list
- Graphic Organizer of your choosing, provided on pages 180–186
- Writing Form: Ways to Earn a Living, page 42

Introduce the Topic

Read aloud and discuss the Ways to Earn a Living text and photos. Explain that jobs change over time for various reasons. As some jobs disappear due to our changing needs, new jobs are created. Point out that some jobs remain the same because they stay in demand.

Read and Respond

Form leveled groups and review the Words to Know lists with each group of students. Instruct each group to read their selection individually, in pairs, or as a group. Have students complete the Reading Comprehension page for their selection.

Write About the Topic

Read aloud the leveled writing prompt for each group. Tell students to use the Graphic Organizer to plan their writing. Direct students to use their Writing Form to respond to their prompt.

Visual Literacy

Writing Form

Nonfiction Reading Practice • EMC 3235 • © Evan-Moor Corp.

Ways to Earn a Living

Have you ever thought about how you want to earn a living as an adult? There are so many jobs to choose from. If you are not quite sure yet which job sounds right for you, not to worry! Jobs are changing all the time.

A switchboard operator used to be needed in order to make calls on a landline phone. This is no longer how phone calls work, however.

Before electric streetlamps were used, lamplighters had the job of manually lighting streetlamps.

Some jobs become unnecessary over time because of advancements in technology. Tech products accomplish the work that people used to do.

Although some jobs are no longer needed, new jobs are created all the time. As technology changes our lives, our needs, wants, and demands change, too.

Nowadays, a machine automatically sets up the pins at the bowling alley. But in the past, people had to do it. It was actually a dangerous job at times!

Ways to Earn a Living

_____
_____
_____
_____
_____
_____
_____
_____
_____
_____
_____
_____
_____
_____
_____
_____
_____

Nonfiction Reading Practice • EMC 3235 • © Evan-Moor Corp.

Words to Know

The Basics of Earning a Living

earn

occupation

pursue

geographical

limitations

supply and demand

robust

universally

Ways to Earn a Living ■

Words to Know

Technology and Jobs

technology

devices

supply and demand

brick-and-mortar

tech

applications

Ways to Earn a Living ■ ■

Words to Know

Creating New Jobs

steadily

strain

demands

switchboard operator

pinboy

app

social media

blogger

Ways to Earn a Living ■ ■ ■

The Basics of Earning a Living

Have you ever thought about all of the ways that people earn a living? For many people, the decision of what occupation to pursue is easy. For others, the decision takes more time to make. Throughout the U.S., there are an array of jobs that people can do. However, not every job is available in every region. There are geographical limitations on where jobs are available.

Supply and Demand

What is a job? A job involves providing goods or services to people who need them. Every economy has a supply-and-demand relationship with goods and services. Demand is the desire or need for goods or services. Supply is the amount that can be provided. A healthy economy has a robust demand for goods and services and an ability to supply them. Providing some goods and services depends on human labor.

Geography

Location can play a role in what types of jobs are available. There are different opportunities to earn a living in different parts of the country. For example, jobs that require the ocean, such as being a fisherman, are not possible for someone who lives in the Great Plains.

On the other hand, there are goods and services that are universally in demand, such as teaching. The chart below lists some of the occupations that exist in the U.S. to meet the demands for goods and services.

Occupation	Geographically Limited or Universal
Commercial Fishing	Geographically Limited
Fishing Boat Repair	Geographically Limited
Crop Farming	Geographically Limited
Automobile Sales	Universal
Ski Instructor	Geographically Limited
Police Officer	Universal

Earning Money to Spend on Goods and Services

When people earn money working, they have money to spend in the economy. People spend their money on goods and services. In an ideal economy, everyone would earn money and spend money continuously so that people would have jobs and money all the time.

   Nonfiction Reading Practice • EMC 3235 • © Evan-Moor Corp.

The Basics of Earning a Living

Fill in the circle by the correct answer. Then write the answers to numbers 3, 4, and 5.

1. Why would a job be "geographically limited" to a specific area?
   Ⓐ The job requires a specific geographical landscape or region.
   Ⓑ The person doing the job needs to have specific skills.
   Ⓒ The good or service provided requires only U.S. dollars.
   Ⓓ The job is in demand everywhere.

2. The word "robust" probably means "_____."
   Ⓐ weak
   Ⓑ strong
   Ⓒ special
   Ⓓ complicated

3. Explain two aspects of a healthy economy.

   _____

   _____

4. List some jobs you know of that are not in the chart and are limited geographically.

   _____

   _____

5. How do goods and services boost the economy?

   _____

   _____

Write About the Topic

Use the Writing Form to write about what you read.

Choose one occupation in the chart that is geographically limited and one that is universal. Explain why this is so.

Technology and Jobs

Technology has made life easier in many ways. People can shop and learn online without ever leaving their homes. We use cameras, phones, Internet devices, fitness tools, and more. While technology has affected how people's needs are met, it has also affected how people earn a living.

Supply and Demand

Many people have jobs that meet other people's wants and needs. The things people need are goods or services. Human labor is required in order to provide goods and services to society. People who work earn money, and then they spend their money on goods and services that other people provide. We spend money on things we need. But what happens to all the stores that sell stuff that people just don't want anymore?

Technology, Goods, and Services

There was a time when people had to go to a video store to rent movies. But today, video rental stores are hard to find. People can watch movies on their electronic and wireless devices. The number of brick-and-mortar bookstores has also decreased, as many people download electronic books. It isn't only the stores, books, and videos that are disappearing, it is also the jobs these stores provided.

There are some services that people depend on that cannot be delivered remotely. Plumbers, for example, must arrive at a physical location to fix a clogged drain, and a childcare provider must be with a child to ensure that the child is safe.

Technology and New Jobs

Technology presents opportunities for new jobs to be created. For example, new technology products need a labor force, as employees are needed to sell the technology product to people and businesses. People are also in need of experts who can answer questions and repair technology products when there are problems. There are many jobs in the technology field. Tech products are constantly being improved and updated. Society is always on the lookout for new forms of technology, and new applications for devices are sold daily.

Technology helps people communicate face-to-face without having to travel long distances.

Although technology has erased the demand for some goods and services, it has offered some new ways of meeting our demands.

Technology and Jobs

Fill in the circle by the correct answer. Then write the answers to numbers 3, 4, and 5.

1. The term "labor force" in the text probably means _____.
   - Ⓐ people who can work
   - Ⓑ people who are strong
   - Ⓒ people who can learn
   - Ⓓ people who like technology

2. The fact that the number of brick-and-mortar stores is decreasing shows that _____.
   - Ⓐ people are more interested in going to the store than shopping online
   - Ⓑ technology products have been in low demand recently
   - Ⓒ society's demands are changing, so supplies need to change, too
   - Ⓓ society's demands are staying the same, but supplies need to change

3. Explain how you could support the view that supply and demand is an endless cycle.

   _____

   _____

4. How does the text support the idea that there is a high demand for tech products?

   _____

   _____

5. Why have some jobs and services been less affected by technology?

   _____

   _____

Write About the Topic

Use the Writing Form to write about what you read.

Has technology helped or harmed people's opportunities to earn a living? Support your argument with details from the text.

Creating New Jobs

Jobs are based on the needs and wants of individuals and society. Many jobs exist today that were not around 60 years ago. Likewise, there were jobs 60 years ago that some people have never heard of today. The world's growing population and improvements in technology have affected the economy and what jobs are available.

The Population and World Resources

The world population has been steadily growing for centuries, and since 1950, it has grown at an even faster rate. There are currently about 7 billion people in the world. It is estimated that in the year 2050, the population will be at 9 billion. This rapid population growth has affected the world's resources. Food, shelter, clothing, education, and clean water are just a few things that people around the world need and want. A larger population puts strain on resources and makes the demand for resources higher. Supplying goods and services that are in demand requires human labor. When the demands change, so do jobs.

Switchboard operator
at work around 1950

Technology

Technology has improved many things in our lives. We can easily communicate over long distances, rely on technology for security and information, take online classes, rent movies, play games, track our fitness, and so much more. It is no wonder that technology products are in high demand. Technology has also affected jobs by allowing people to work from home and to take jobs that are out of the state (and even out of the country). The chart below shows some of the jobs that have been phased out and some new jobs that have been created.

Jobs needed in 1950 that were not needed in 2017	Jobs needed in 2017 that were not needed in 1950
Switchboard operator: wrote phone numbers and flipped switches to allow long-distance phone calls	App developer: creates apps for devices such as smartphones and tablets
Milkman: delivered fresh milk to people's homes	Social media marketer: identifies customer needs and addresses concerns on social media
Pinboy: set up pins in bowling alley lanes	Blogger: writes informative or entertaining online narrations

    Nonfiction Reading Practice • EMC 3235 • © Evan-Moor Corp.

Creating New Jobs

Fill in the circle by the correct answer. Then write the answers to numbers 3, 4, and 5.

1. From the chart, you can make the inference that _____.
   Ⓐ switchboard operators are now doing their jobs for mobile calls
   Ⓑ long-distance calls are no longer being made on landline phones
   Ⓒ switchboards aren't necessary to make long-distance calls now
   Ⓓ the U.S. no longer has a need for phones of any kind

2. How can we estimate what the world population will be in 2050?
   Ⓐ We know what the current world population is.
   Ⓑ There is data from 2050 that informs us of the population.
   Ⓒ We can assume that the population will not grow very much.
   Ⓓ We can estimate based on the growth rate from recent decades.

3. Explain why jobs change when demand changes.

   _____

   _____

4. How does population growth affect the kinds of jobs that are needed?

   _____

   _____

5. Based on the chart, what's so different about the types of jobs in 1950 and 2017?

   _____

   _____

Write About the Topic

Use the Writing Form to write about what you read.

Explain how jobs will be different 60 years from now and why, and predict what some future jobs will be. Use text details.

Earth's Water

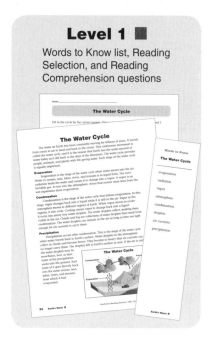
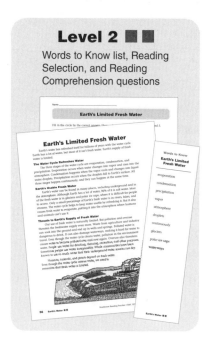
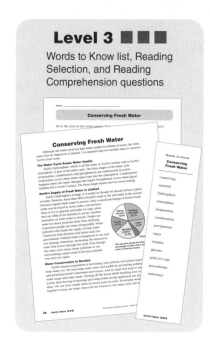
Assemble the Unit

Reproduce and distribute one copy for each student:

- Visual Literacy page: Earth's Water, page 51
- Level 1, 2, or 3 Reading Selection and Reading Comprehension page and the corresponding Words to Know list
- Graphic Organizer of your choosing, provided on pages 180–186
- Writing Form: Earth's Water, page 52

Visual Literacy

Introduce the Topic

Read aloud and discuss The Water Cycle diagram. Explain that the water cycle renews water with every stage. Tell students that Earth has not gained or lost any water for billions of years, but our water supply is limited because of threats such as pollution.

Read and Respond

Form leveled groups and review the Words to Know lists with each group of students. Instruct each group to read their selection individually, in pairs, or as a group. Have students complete the Reading Comprehension page for their selection.

Writing Form

Write About the Topic

Read aloud the leveled writing prompt for each group. Tell students to use the Graphic Organizer to plan their writing. Direct students to use their Writing Form to respond to their prompt.

Earth's Water

1. Heat from the sun causes liquid water to evaporate from Earth's surface and from bodies of water.

2. Liquid water evaporates into an invisible gas called water vapor.

3. Water vapor rises above Earth where the air is cooler.

4. Water vapor cools and condenses. Tiny water droplets are formed in clouds.

5. Eventually these droplets become heavy enough to fall from the clouds to Earth as precipitation. Depending on the temperature, precipitation can fall as rain, snow, sleet, or hail.

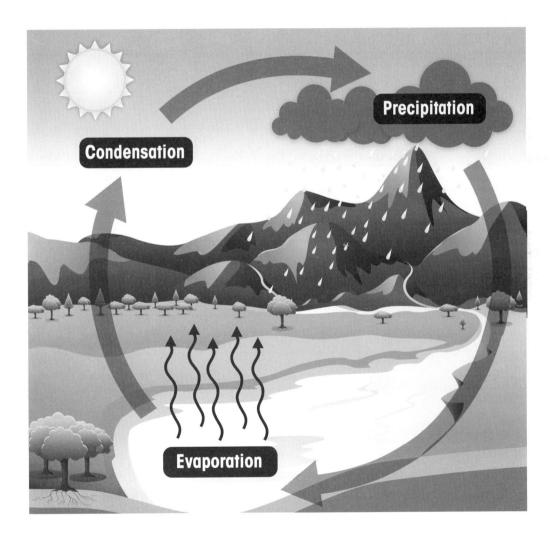

After the precipitation is back on Earth, it will eventually evaporate, thus continuing the water cycle. The amount of water on Earth doesn't change. The water is just reused again and again.

Name _____

Earth's Water

_____

_____

_____

_____

_____

_____

_____

_____

_____

_____

_____

_____

_____

_____

_____

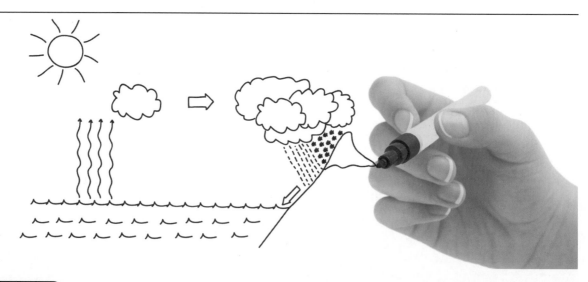

Words to Know	Words to Know	Words to Know
The Water Cycle	**Earth's Limited Fresh Water**	**Conserving Fresh Water**
evaporation	evaporation	conserving
radiation	condensation	essential
vapor	precipitation	hydrosphere
atmosphere	vapor	atmosphere
condensation	atmosphere	evaporation
droplets	droplets	condensation
air currents	continuously	precipitation
precipitation	glaciers	vapor
	polar ice caps	droplets
	waterways	glaciers
		polar ice caps
		groundwater
		waterways
Earth's Water ▪	**Earth's Water** ▪▪	**Earth's Water** ▪▪▪

© Evan-Moor Corp. • EMC 3235 • Nonfiction Reading Practice   **Words to Know**   53

The Water Cycle

The water on Earth has been constantly moving for billions of years. It travels from ocean to air to land and back to the ocean. This continuous movement is called the water cycle, and it is the reason that Earth has the same amount of water today as it did back in the days of the dinosaurs. The water cycle provides people, animals, and plants with life-giving water. Each stage of the water cycle is equally important.

Evaporation

Evaporation is the stage of the water cycle when water moves into the air. Water in oceans, seas, lakes, rivers, and streams is in liquid form. The sun's radiation heats the water and causes it to change into a vapor. A vapor is an invisible gas. It rises into the atmosphere. Areas that receive more heat from the sun experience more evaporation.

Condensation

Condensation is the stage of the water cycle that follows evaporation. In this stage, vapor changes back into a liquid while it is still in the air. Vapor in the atmosphere moves to different regions of Earth. When vapor moves to cooler regions, it also cools. Cooling causes vapor to change back into a liquid. It turns into many tiny water droplets. The water droplets collect, making them visible in the air. Clouds and fog are collections of water droplets that result from condensation. The water droplets can remain in the air as long as they are light enough for air currents to carry them.

Precipitation

Precipitation occurs after condensation. This is the stage of the water cycle when water travels back to Earth's surface. Water droplets in the atmosphere collect in clouds and become heavy. They become so heavy that air currents can no longer carry them. The droplets fall to Earth's surface as rain. If the air is cold, the water droplets may be snowflakes, hail, or sleet. Some of the precipitation soaks into the ground. And some of it goes directly back into the same oceans, seas, lakes, rivers, and streams from which it had evaporated.

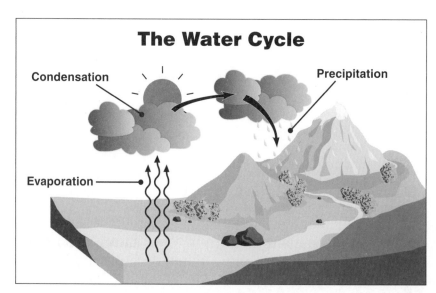

The Water Cycle

Condensation

Precipitation

Evaporation

    Nonfiction Reading Practice • EMC 3235 • © Evan-Moor Corp.

The Water Cycle

Fill in the circle by the correct answer. Then write the answers to numbers 3, 4, and 5.

1. One of the main ideas in the text is that _____.
   - Ⓐ precipitation can be rain, snow, hail, or sleet
   - Ⓑ we drink the same water today that dinosaurs drank
   - Ⓒ condensation follows the evaporation stage
   - Ⓓ all stages of the water cycle are equally important

2. How is evaporation similar to condensation?
   - Ⓐ In both stages water changes its form.
   - Ⓑ Both stages involve rain and clouds.
   - Ⓒ They are more important than precipitation.
   - Ⓓ In both stages, the ocean plays an important role.

3. Why is the precipitation stage needed for the water cycle to work?

   _____

   _____

4. Explain how the diagram helped you understand the water cycle.

   _____

   _____

5. What do you think would happen if the water cycle stopped working?

   _____

   _____

Write About the Topic

Use the Writing Form to write about what you read.

Write about the water cycle. Describe what it is and how it works. Use details from the text in your description.

Earth's Limited Fresh Water

Earth's water has refreshed itself for billions of years with the water cycle. Earth has a lot of water, but most of it isn't fresh water. Earth's supply of fresh water is limited.

The Water Cycle Refreshes Water

The three stages of the water cycle are evaporation, condensation, and precipitation. Evaporation occurs when water changes into vapor and rises into the atmosphere. Condensation happens when the vapor cools and changes into liquid water droplets. Precipitation occurs when the droplets fall to Earth's surface. All three stages happen continuously, and they can happen at the same time.

Earth's Usable Fresh Water

Earth's water can be found in many places, including underground and in the atmosphere. Although Earth has a lot of water, 96% of it is salt water. Most of the fresh water is in glaciers and polar ice caps, where it is difficult for people to access. Only a small percentage of Earth's fresh water is in rivers, lakes, and streams. The water cycle helps to keep water usable by refreshing it. But it also causes fresh water to evaporate, putting it into the atmosphere where humans and animals can't use it.

Threats to Earth's Supply of Fresh Water

Our use of fresh water is naturally limited. But pollution and overuse threaten the freshwater supply even more. Waste from agriculture and industry can soak into the ground and end up in wells and springs. Polluted water is dangerous to drink. It can also damage waterways, making it hard for water to travel. Even though the water cycle cleans water, pollution in the environment causes water to become polluted over and over again. Overuse also threatens water. People use water for drinking, cleaning, recreation, and other purposes. Sometimes people use water irresponsibly. Whole communities have been known to use so much water that their underground water sources run dry.

Humans, animals, and plants depend on fresh water. Even though the water cycle renews water, we need to remember that fresh water is limited.

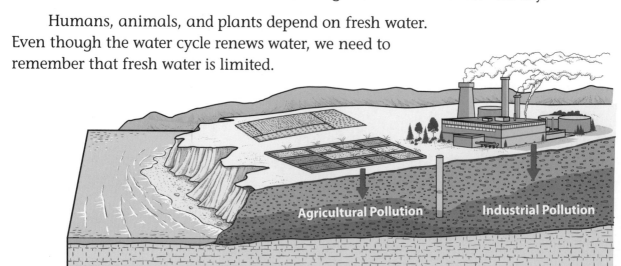

Agricultural Pollution   Industrial Pollution

Name _____

Earth's Limited Fresh Water

Fill in the circle by the correct answer. Then write the answers to numbers 3, 4, and 5.

1. Why is it important that more than 96% of Earth's water is salt water?
   - Ⓐ This fact shows how many marine animals depend on salt water.
   - Ⓑ It shows that humans, animals, and plants are able to use most of Earth's water for survival.
   - Ⓒ We do not have to be concerned at all about water pollution in salt water.
   - Ⓓ It means that we can't use most of Earth's water for survival.

2. What inference can be made about polluted water?
   - Ⓐ It smells bad but is probably safe to drink.
   - Ⓑ Drinking it could harm people and animals.
   - Ⓒ The water cycle is a solution for polluted water.
   - Ⓓ It is found only in wells and springs.

3. Would it be better if fresh water did not evaporate? Explain why or why not.

   _____

   _____

4. Write a main idea from the text and a detail that supports it.

   _____

   _____

5. Explain what water overuse is and why it's a problem.

   _____

   _____

Write About the Topic

Use the Writing Form to write about what you read.

Explain the relationship between the water cycle and Earth's supply of fresh water. Use details from the text in your explanation.

Conserving Fresh Water

Although the water cycle has kept water usable for billions of years, the fresh water that we depend on is limited. It is essential that we consider ways to conserve Earth's fresh water.

The Water Cycle Keeps Water Usable

Earth's hydrosphere, which is all the water on Earth's surface and in Earth's atmosphere, is part of the water cycle. The three stages of the water cycle (evaporation, condensation, and precipitation) are continuously in action. Evaporation occurs when water vapor rises into the atmosphere. Condensation happens when the vapor changes into liquid. Precipitation occurs when liquid droplets fall to Earth's surface. The three stages repeat and are never-ending.

Earth's Supply of Fresh Water Is Limited

Earth's hydrosphere is huge, so it seems as though we should all have plenty of water. However, more than 96% of Earth's water is the salt water in the oceans. Humans require fresh water to survive. Only a small percentage of Earth's fresh water can be found in rivers, lakes, and streams. Most of it is in glaciers and polar ice caps, areas that are difficult for humans to access. Another limitation on fresh water is overuse. People use water for many purposes other than drinking. Sometimes people use water irresponsibly. Water pollution also limits the supply of fresh water. Chemicals from factories and farms soak into groundwater. Polluted water is dangerous to use and can damage waterways, decreasing the amount of water that moves through the cycle. Even though the water cycle cleans water, pollution in our surroundings causes water to become polluted over and over again.

This pie chart shows the daily percentage of water that is typically used in American homes.

Water Conservation Is Needed

Earth's human population is increasing, and animals and plants require fresh water, too. We must keep water clean and usable by preventing pollution and protecting Earth's waterways and oceans. And we must find ways to decrease water usage and water waste. Turning off the faucet while brushing your teeth (rather than leaving it running) and using water-saving appliances are just two ideas. We can have usable water for many years to come. If everyone works together to keep our water clean and not overuse it, the water cycle will do the rest.

Nonfiction Reading Practice • EMC 3235 • © Evan-Moor Corp.

Conserving Fresh Water

Fill in the circle by the correct answer. Then write the answers to numbers 3, 4, and 5.

1. According to the pie chart, _____.
   Ⓐ leaks cause the heaviest use of water in typical homes
   Ⓑ very few American homes use water for flushing the toilet
   Ⓒ we know how more than 90% of water is used every day
   Ⓓ we get most of our household water from precipitation

2. How can the information in the pie chart help us to conserve water?
   Ⓐ The chart can make people aware of how much water they use or overuse.
   Ⓑ We can see that clothes washers should be banned.
   Ⓒ The chart shows specific houses that overuse water.
   Ⓓ We can use the information to increase the supply of fresh water.

3. What steps would you recommend to people who want to conserve water?

   _____

   _____

4. Explain how the author uses each paragraph to support each bold-text main idea.

   _____

   _____

5. Why can't we rely on the water cycle alone to have enough fresh water?

   _____

   _____

Write About the Topic

Use the Writing Form to write about what you read.

Did the author succeed at proving that water conservation is necessary? Write an argument for why or why not. Use examples.

Matter and Mass

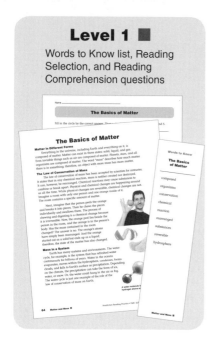

Level 1 ■
Words to Know list, Reading Selection, and Reading Comprehension questions

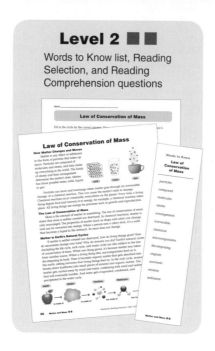

Level 2 ■ ■
Words to Know list, Reading Selection, and Reading Comprehension questions

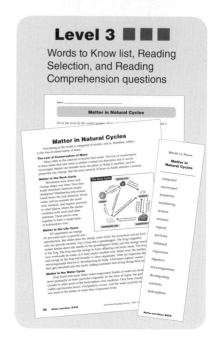

Level 3 ■ ■ ■
Words to Know list, Reading Selection, and Reading Comprehension questions

Assemble the Unit

Reproduce and distribute one copy for each student:

- Visual Literacy page: Matter Moves Through Cycles, page 61
- Level 1, 2, or 3 Reading Selection and Reading Comprehension page and the corresponding Words to Know list
- Graphic Organizer of your choosing, provided on pages 180–186
- Writing Form: Matter and Mass, page 62

Introduce the Topic

Read aloud and discuss the Matter Moves Through Cycles diagram. Explain that the total mass of the universe never changes, but its matter can rearrange. Point out that matter can go through chemical changes and new substances can be created, but mass remains constant even when matter looks different.

Read and Respond

Form leveled groups and review the Words to Know lists with each group of students. Instruct each group to read their selection individually, in pairs, or as a group. Have students complete the Reading Comprehension page for their selection.

Write About the Topic

Read aloud the leveled writing prompt for each group. Tell students to use the Graphic Organizer to plan their writing. Direct students to use their Writing Form to respond to their prompt.

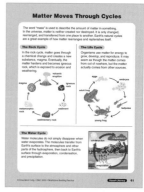

Visual Literacy

Writing Form

Nonfiction Reading Practice • EMC 3235 • © Evan-Moor Corp.

Matter Moves Through Cycles

The word "mass" is used to describe the amount of matter in something. In the universe, matter is neither created nor destroyed. It is only changed, rearranged, and transferred from one place to another. Earth's natural cycles are a great example of how matter rearranges and replenishes itself.

The Rock Cycle

In the rock cycle, matter goes through a chemical change and creates a new substance, magma. Eventually, the matter hardens and becomes igneous rock, which is exposed to erosion and weathering.

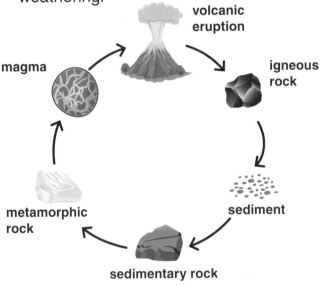

The Life Cycle

Organisms use matter for energy to grow, develop, and reproduce. It may seem as though the matter comes from out of nowhere, but the matter actually comes from other sources.

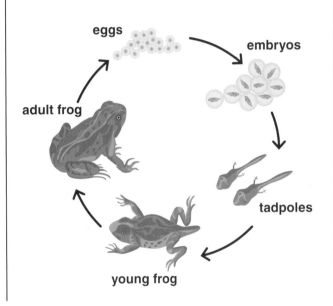

The Water Cycle

Water molecules do not simply disappear when water evaporates. The molecules transfer from Earth's surface to the atmosphere and other parts of the hydrosphere, then back to Earth's surface through evaporation, condensation, and precipitation.

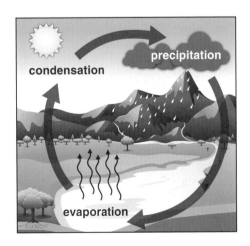

Matter and Mass

_____

_____

_____

_____

_____

_____

_____

_____

_____

_____

_____

_____

_____

_____

_____

_____

_____

Words to Know

The Basics of Matter

composed

organisms

conservation

chemical

reaction

rearranged

substances

reversible

hydrosphere

Matter and Mass ▪

Words to Know

Law of Conservation of Mass

particles

composed

molecules

atoms

arrangement

irreversible

chemical

microorganisms

decomposing

organic

nutrients

erosion

sediment

Matter and Mass ▪ ▪

Words to Know

Matter in Natural Cycles

composed

rearranged

properties

weathering

erosion

mineral

organic

particles

sediment

organisms

digestive

microorganisms

decomposing

nutrients

hydrosphere

Matter and Mass ▪ ▪ ▪

The Basics of Matter

Matter in Different Forms

Everything in the universe, including Earth and everything on it, is composed of matter. Matter can exist in three states: solid, liquid, and gas. Even invisible things such as air are composed of matter. Planets, stars, and all organisms are composed of matter. The word "mass" describes how much matter there is in something; therefore, an object with more mass has more matter.

The Law of Conservation of Mass

The law of conservation of mass has been accepted by scientists for centuries. It states that in any chemical reaction, mass is neither created nor destroyed. It can, however, be rearranged. Chemical reactions may cause substances to combine or break apart. Physical and chemical changes are happening around us all the time. While physical changes are reversible, chemical changes are not. Imagine a room with only one person and one orange inside of it. The room contains a specific amount of matter.

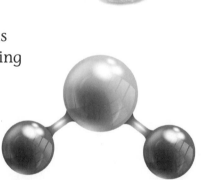

Next, imagine that the person peels the orange and breaks it into pieces. Then he chews the pieces individually and swallows them. The process of chewing and digesting is a chemical change because it is irreversible. Now, the orange peel lies beside the person in the room, and the orange is in the person's body. Has the mass contained in the room changed? The answer is no. The orange's atoms have simply been rearranged. And the orange started out as a solid but ends up as a liquid; therefore, the state of the matter has also changed.

Mass in a System

Earth has many systems and environments. The water cycle, for example, is the system that has refreshed water continuously for billions of years. Water in the oceans evaporates, moves within the hydrosphere, condenses, forms clouds, and falls to Earth's surface as precipitation. Depending on the climate, the precipitation can take the form of ice, water, or snow. Or, the water could hang in the air as fog. The water cycle is just one example of the role of the law of conservation of mass on Earth.

A water molecule is composed of two hydrogen atoms and one oxygen atom.

     Nonfiction Reading Practice • EMC 3235 • © Evan-Moor Corp.

The Basics of Matter

Fill in the circle by the correct answer. Then write the answers to numbers 3, 4, and 5.

1. Earth has the same amount of water as it did billions of years ago because _____.
   - Ⓐ water only moves within the ocean
   - Ⓑ water does not have a mass, so it's not as heavy
   - Ⓒ even invisible things such as air are made of matter
   - Ⓓ of the law of conservation of mass

2. _____ is an example of a chemical reaction.
   - Ⓐ Water changing into ice
   - Ⓑ An egg becoming hard-boiled
   - Ⓒ A frying pan heating up
   - Ⓓ Folding a dollar bill

3. If the person had eaten the orange peel, too, would the mass in the room have changed? Explain why or why not.

   _____

   _____

4. Does the state of matter in an object affect the mass? Explain why or why not.

   _____

   _____

5. When substances combine or break apart, what is happening to the matter?

   _____

   _____

Write About the Topic

Use the Writing Form to write about what you read.

> Explain how the law of conservation of mass relates to matter as it moves through the water cycle. Use details and examples.

Law of Conservation of Mass

How Matter Changes and Moves

Matter is any object or substance in the form of particles that takes up space. Particles are composed of molecules and atoms, and they make up everything in the world. The kinds of atoms and their arrangement determine the matter's state. Matter has three possible states: solid, liquid, or gas.

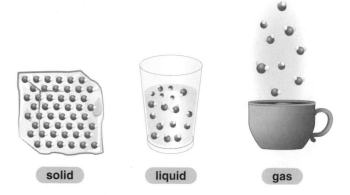

solid   liquid   gas

Particles can move and rearrange when matter goes through an irreversible change, or a chemical reaction. This can cause the matter's state to change. Chemical reactions occur constantly, everywhere on the planet. Every time a living thing digests food and converts it to energy, for example, a chemical reaction takes place. All living things use energy for processes such as growth and reproduction.

The Law of Conservation of Mass

Mass is the amount of matter in something. The law of conservation of mass states that mass is neither created nor destroyed. In chemical reactions, matter is only rearranged. The properties of matter (such as shape and color) can change, and can be converted into energy. When a person eats a celery stick, it's a solid that becomes a liquid in the stomach. Its mass does not change.

Matter in Earth's Natural Cycles

If matter is neither created nor destroyed, how do living things grow? How do mountains change over time? Why do streams run dry? Earth's natural cycles (including the life cycle, rock cycle, and water cycle) are also subject to the law of conservation of mass. When one thing grows, it's because matter was taken from another source. When a living thing dies, microorganisms feed on it, decomposing its body. Then it becomes organic matter that gets absorbed into the earth, adding nutrients that living things feed on. In the rock cycle, erosion breaks down landforms into small pieces of mineral and organic matter. The matter gets carried away by wind and water, combining with sand and sediment that will eventually harden. And water gets evaporated, condensed, and precipitated in the water cycle.

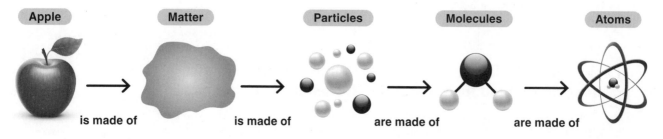

Apple → Matter → Particles → Molecules → Atoms

is made of   is made of   are made of   are made of

    Nonfiction Reading Practice • EMC 3235 • © Evan-Moor Corp.

Law of Conservation of Mass

Fill in the circle by the correct answer. Then write the answers to numbers 3, 4, and 5.

1. When a living thing digests food, the _____.
   Ⓐ chemical reaction does not occur
   Ⓑ food's matter is rearranged
   Ⓒ living thing's matter is rearranged
   Ⓓ law of conservation of mass doesn't apply

2. When a landform or a living thing gets smaller, it's because _____.
   Ⓐ new matter formed in another place
   Ⓑ Earth's mass decreased
   Ⓒ matter was used up and disappeared
   Ⓓ matter was transferred from it to another place

3. What do microorganisms have in common with erosion?

   _____

   _____

4. Explain how the law of conservation of mass allows Earth's cycles to continue.

   _____

   _____

5. How are humans and their belongings subject to the law of conservation of mass?

   _____

   _____

Write About the Topic

Use the Writing Form to write about what you read.

Elaborate on why Earth's total mass will never change.
Use details from the text, and provide your own examples.

Matter in Natural Cycles

Everything in the world is composed of matter, and is, therefore, subject to the law of conservation of mass.

The Law of Conservation of Mass

Mass refers to the amount of matter that exists. The law of conservation of mass states that new mass is neither created nor destroyed, but it can be rearranged. Matter can transfer from one place or thing to another, and its properties can change. But the total amount of mass on Earth remains constant.

Matter in the Rock Cycle

Mountains wear down and change shape over time. Does that tough mountain material simply disappear? Weathering and erosion break down the rock material. Wind, water, and ice transfer the small rock, mineral, and organic particles to other places, where the matter combines with sand and other sediment. These pieces come together to form a tough mass of sedimentary rock.

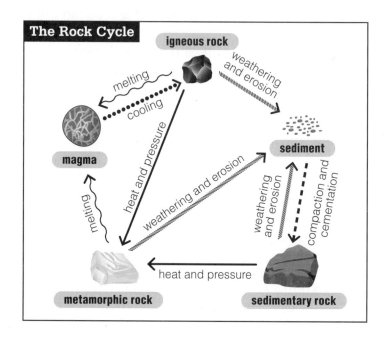

The Rock Cycle

igneous rock

melting
cooling

weathering and erosion

magma

heat and pressure

melting

weathering and erosion

sediment

weathering and erosion

compaction and cementation

metamorphic rock

heat and pressure

sedimentary rock

Matter in the Life Cycle

All organisms use energy for processes such as growth and reproduction. But where does the energy come from? An ecosystem and its food web can provide answers. Say a frog eats a grasshopper. The frog's digestive system breaks down the matter in the grasshopper's body, and the energy transfers to the frog. The frog uses the energy to form offspring and more mass. The frog may eventually be eaten, or it may expire another way. Either way, the matter and energy in the frog will transfer to other organisms. After an organism dies, microorganisms feed on it, decomposing its body. It becomes organic matter that gets absorbed into the earth, adding nutrients that living things feed on.

Matter in the Water Cycle

Does Earth lose mass when water evaporates? Bodies of water are broken down gradually as water particles evaporate. In the form of vapor, the particles transfer to other parts of the hydrosphere and condense. They form clouds that are visible and become heavy. Precipitation occurs, and the water particles find their way back to the bodies of water they evaporated from.

Matter in Natural Cycles

Fill in the circle by the correct answer. Then write the answers to numbers 3, 4, and 5.

1. An organism growing bigger is evidence that _____.
   Ⓐ energy that didn't exist on Earth before has transferred to the organism
   Ⓑ the organism has created matter that didn't exist before
   Ⓒ matter has transferred to the organism from another place
   Ⓓ the organism has not gained or lost any mass

2. According to the text, _____.
   Ⓐ the matter in sedimentary rock eventually transfers to another place
   Ⓑ igneous rock cannot break down as other rocks can
   Ⓒ weathering and erosion is the only way rock matter changes
   Ⓓ sedimentary rock is not composed of matter

3. Explain how the law of conservation of mass makes it possible for the grasshopper to help the frog survive.

   _____

   _____

4. What would happen if food matter simply disappeared after organisms ate? Explain how Earth would be different.

   _____

   _____

5. Why is the law of conservation of mass essential for all of the natural cycles to work?

   _____

   _____

Write About the Topic

Use the Writing Form to write about what you read.

> Compare and contrast how matter moves through the three cycles mentioned in the text. Use details and examples.

Relationships in Nature

Level 1 ■
Words to Know list, Reading Selection, and Reading Comprehension questions

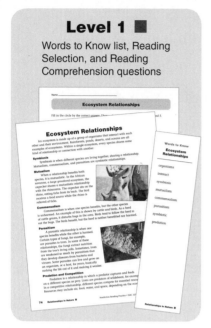

Level 2 ■ ■
Words to Know list, Reading Selection, and Reading Comprehension questions

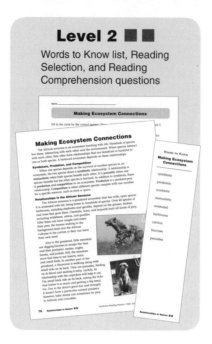

Level 3 ■ ■ ■
Words to Know list, Reading Selection, and Reading Comprehension questions

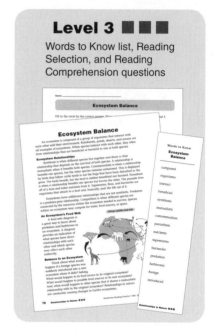

Assemble the Unit

Reproduce and distribute one copy for each student:

- Visual Literacy page: Relationships in Nature, page 71
- Level 1, 2, or 3 Reading Selection and Reading Comprehension page and the corresponding Words to Know list
- Graphic Organizer of your choosing, provided on pages 180–186
- Writing Form: Relationships in Nature, page 72

Introduce the Topic

Read aloud and discuss the Relationships in Nature text and photographs. Explain that all ecosystems have different species that interact with each other and their environments. Point out that different relationships exist within one ecosystem and that they might be beneficial or harmful or have no effect at all on a species.

Read and Respond

Form leveled groups and review the Words to Know lists with each group of students. Instruct each group to read their selection individually, in pairs, or as a group. Have students complete the Reading Comprehension page for their selection.

Write About the Topic

Read aloud the leveled writing prompt for each group. Tell students to use the Graphic Organizer to plan their writing. Direct students to use their Writing Form to respond to their prompt.

Visual Literacy

Writing Form

Nonfiction Reading Practice • EMC 3235 • © Evan-Moor Corp.

Relationships in Nature

In an ecosystem, different species share close relationships with each other and their environment.

Mutualism is a symbiotic relationship in which two species benefit each other.

The clown fish makes its home in the sea anemone. The sea anemone provides protection to the clown fish. The clown fish eats the anemone's dead tentacles and lures prey for the anemone.

Parasitism is a relationship in which one species benefits and one is harmed.

Some forms of fungi attach to plants and take nutrients away from the plant. This makes the plant weaker but the fungi stronger.

Predation is a relationship in which a predator hunts and eats prey.

A lion in the African savanna depends on prey as a food source.

Competition is a relationship in which different species depend on the same resource within an ecosystem.

The hyena and African vulture both depend on carrion as a major food source in the African savanna.

Name _____

Relationships in Nature

_____
_____
_____
_____
_____
_____
_____
_____
_____
_____
_____
_____
_____
_____
_____
_____
_____

Words to Know	Words to Know	Words to Know
Ecosystem Relationships	**Making Ecosystem Connections**	**Ecosystem Balance**
organisms	symbiosis	composed
interact	predation	organisms
symbiosis	symbiotic	interact
mutualism	mutualistic	beneficial
commensalism	animated	symbiosis
parasitism	herbivores	mutualistic
symbiotic	carrion	commensalism
predation	burrows	parasitism
	parasites	nutrients
		tapeworms
		barnacles
		predation
		herbivores
		foreign
		introduced
Relationships in Nature ■	**Relationships in Nature** ■ ■	**Relationships in Nature** ■ ■ ■

Ecosystem Relationships

An ecosystem is made up of a group of organisms that interact with each other and their environment. Rainforests, ponds, deserts, and oceans are all examples of ecosystems. Within a single ecosystem, every species shares some kind of relationship or connection with another.

Symbiosis

Symbiosis is when different species are living together, sharing a relationship. Mutualism, commensalism, and parasitism are symbiotic relationships.

Mutualism

When a relationship benefits both species, it is mutualistic. In the African savanna, a large grassland ecosystem, the oxpecker shares a mutualistic relationship with the rhinoceros. The oxpecker sits on the rhino, eating ticks from its back. The bird receives a food source while the rhino is relieved of ticks.

Commensalism

Commensalism is when one species benefits, but the other species is unharmed. An example of this is shown by cattle and birds. As a herd of cattle grazes, it disturbs bugs in the area. Birds tend to follow the herd to eat the bugs. The birds benefit, but the herd is neither benefitted nor harmed.

Parasitism

A parasitic relationship is when one species benefits while the other is harmed. Certain types of fungi, for example, are parasites to trees. In some of these relationships, the fungi extract nutrition from the tree's living cells. Sometimes, trees are weakened so much by parasitism that they develop diseases from bacteria and viruses. Some parasites can live and grow on an organism, or a host, for years, basically sucking the life out of it and making it weaker.

Predation and Competition

Predation is a relationship in which a predator captures and feeds on a different species as prey. Lions are predators of wildebeest, for example. In a competitive relationship, different species compete for essential resources. Resources may include air, food, water, and space, depending on the ecosystem.

Name _____

Ecosystem Relationships

Fill in the circle by the correct answer. Then write the answers to numbers 3, 4, and 5.

1. In the second photo within the text, the _____.
   Ⓐ tree is benefitted by the fungus's living cells
   Ⓑ fungus is surviving off of the tree's living cells
   Ⓒ fungus is growing on the tree, but the tree is unharmed
   Ⓓ tree and the fungus are sharing a mutualistic relationship

2. When birds follow cattle to find bugs to eat, the disturbed bugs are _____.
   Ⓐ benefitted
   Ⓑ parasitic
   Ⓒ predators
   Ⓓ prey

3. What would happen if the tree in a tree-fungi parasitic relationship suddenly died? Explain why this would happen.

   _____

   _____

4. In your opinion, which is the worst kind of relationship for an organism? Explain why.

   _____

   _____

5. Would it be possible for an organism <u>not</u> to be part of an ecosystem relationship? Why or why not?

   _____

   _____

Write About the Topic

Use the Writing Form to write about what you read.

Describe an ecosystem you studied or know about and identify relationships from the text that are in it. Give specific examples.

Making Ecosystem Connections

The African savanna is an ecosystem bursting with life. Hundreds of species live there, interacting with each other and the environment. When species interact with each other, they often form relationships that are beneficial or harmful to one or both species. A balanced ecosystem depends on these relationships.

Symbiosis, Predation, and Competition

When one species depends on the survival of another species in an ecosystem, the two species share a **symbiotic** relationship. A relationship is **mutualistic** when both species benefit each other. It is **parasitic** when one species benefits but the other species is harmed. In addition to symbiosis, there is **predation** and **competition** in an ecosystem. **Predation** is a predator-prey relationship. **Competition** is when different species compete with one another for a specific resource, such as food or space.

Relationships in the African Savanna

The African savanna is a grassland ecosystem that has wide, open spaces. It is animated with life, being home to hundreds of species. Over 40 species of herbivores, including elephants and giraffes, depend on the grasses, bushes, and trees that grow there. Cheetahs, lions, and leopards hunt all kinds of prey, including wildebeest, zebras, and gazelles. After these cats have caught and eaten their prey, the hyenas waiting in the background must race the African vultures to the carrion so they can have their own meal.

Also in the grassland, little meerkats are digging burrows to escape the heat and their predators: snakes, eagles, hawks, and jackals. Still, the meerkats must find time to eat insects, mice, and small birds. In another part of the grassland, a rhinoceros is walking along with small ticks on its back. They are parasites, feeding on its blood and making it itchy. Luckily, its relationship with the oxpeckers will help it out. The small birds ride on its back, eating the ticks that bother it so much and getting a big meal, too. Due to the rhino's great size and strength, it doesn't have a particular animal predator. However, baby rhinos can sometimes be prey to wildcats and crocodiles.

Name _____

Making Ecosystem Connections

Fill in the circle by the correct answer. Then write the answers to numbers 3, 4, and 5.

1. Which sentence describes a mutualistic relationship?
   - Ⓐ Bees use flowers for pollen to make nectar, and flowers use bees to reproduce.
   - Ⓑ Vultures and hyenas compete for carrion as a food source in the savanna.
   - Ⓒ Mosquitos land on animals and feed on their blood for nutrients.
   - Ⓓ Rattle, an herb, attaches to grass roots and takes nutrients away from the grass.

2. Which of the following animals can be prey, according to the text?
   - Ⓐ jackal
   - Ⓑ eagle
   - Ⓒ meerkat
   - Ⓓ vulture

3. What would happen if two species were in competition, and one was more successful?

   _____

   _____

4. Is ecosystem balance important? How could eagles affect the mouse population?

   _____

   _____

5. Explain what it means for a species to be "benefitted" or "harmed" in an ecosystem.

   _____

   _____

Write About the Topic

Use the Writing Form to write about what you read.

Compare the roles that the meerkat and the rhino play in their relationships with other species. Use details from the text.

Ecosystem Balance

An ecosystem is composed of a group of organisms that interact with each other and their environment. Rainforests, ponds, deserts, and oceans are all examples of ecosystems. When species interact with each other, they often form relationships that are beneficial or harmful to one or both species.

Ecosystem Relationships

Symbiosis is when different species live together and share a close relationship that depends on the survival of both species. A relationship is mutualistic when it benefits both species. Commensalism is when a relationship benefits one species, but the other species remains unharmed. This is displayed by birds that follow cattle herds to eat the bugs that have been disturbed in the grass. The birds benefit, but the herd is neither benefitted nor harmed. Parasitism is when a relationship benefits one species but harms the other. The parasite lives off of a host and takes nutrients from it. Tapeworms, fleas, and barnacles are organisms that attach to a host and, basically, suck the life out of it.

Ecosystems have additional relationships that are not symbiotic. Predation is a predator-prey relationship. Competition is when different species are connected by the resources within the ecosystem needed to survive. Species within an ecosystem may compete for water, food sources, or space.

An Ecosystem's Food Web

A food web diagram is a great way to learn about predation and herbivores in an ecosystem. A diagram provides an indication of what species have direct relationships with each other and which species may affect each other indirectly.

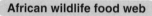

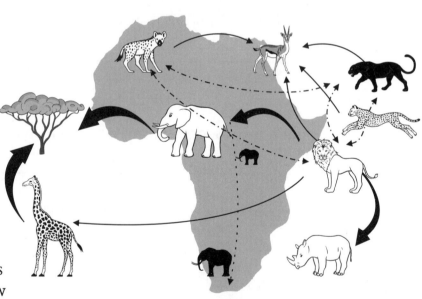

African wildlife food web

Balance in an Ecosystem

Think about what would happen if a foreign species was suddenly introduced into a new ecosystem where it didn't belong. What would happen to its food source in its original ecosystem? What would happen to possible food sources in its new ecosystem? And, what would happen to other species that it shares a mutualistic relationship with in the original ecosystem? Relationships in nature are constantly causing changes in Earth's ecosystems.

Ecosystem Balance

Fill in the circle by the correct answer. Then write the answers to numbers 3, 4, and 5.

1. According to the diagram, _____.
   - Ⓐ giraffes have no predators
   - Ⓑ lions feed on their own species
   - Ⓒ cheetahs and rhinoceroses compete with each other
   - Ⓓ giraffes and elephants compete with each other

2. The last paragraph of the text provides questions that _____.
   - Ⓐ the author and readers should know the exact answers to
   - Ⓑ encourage thinking about an organism's role in its ecosystem
   - Ⓒ are related to a situation that is absolutely impossible
   - Ⓓ are meant to make the reader think mainly about parasitism

3. Explain why predation and competition are not considered symbiosis.

   _____

   _____

4. What would happen if only one species at the top of the food chain were to disappear?

   _____

   _____

5. According to the diagram, which animals are in competition with each other?

   _____

   _____

Write About the Topic

Use the Writing Form to write about what you read.

Write about why the balance of different species in an ecosystem is important. Use details and examples.

The Sun and Stars

Level 1 ■
Words to Know list, Reading Selection, and Reading Comprehension questions

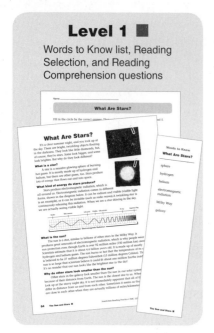

Level 2 ■ ■
Words to Know list, Reading Selection, and Reading Comprehension questions

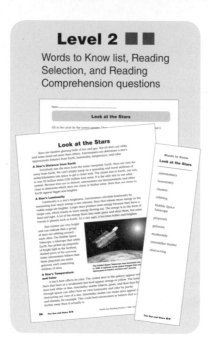

Level 3 ■ ■ ■
Words to Know list, Reading Selection, and Reading Comprehension questions

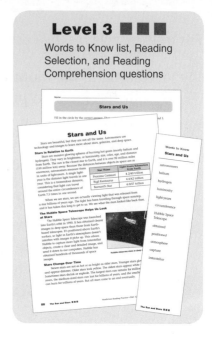

Assemble the Unit

Reproduce and distribute one copy for each student:

- Visual Literacy page: The Sun and Stars, page 81
- Level 1, 2, or 3 Reading Selection and Reading Comprehension page and the corresponding Words to Know list
- Graphic Organizer of your choosing, provided on pages 180–186
- Writing Form: The Sun and Stars, page 82

Introduce the Topic

Read aloud and discuss the text and photographs of the stars, the sun, and the Hubble Space Telescope. Explain that stars vary in their heat, size, age, brightness, color, and distance from Earth. Point out that the sun is the only star in our solar system. Ask students if the sun is the biggest, brightest star they have ever seen in the sky.

Read and Respond

Form leveled groups and review the Words to Know lists with each group of students. Instruct each group to read their selection individually, in pairs, or as a group. Have students complete the Reading Comprehension page for their selection.

Write About the Topic

Read aloud the leveled writing prompt for each group. Tell students to use the Graphic Organizer to plan their writing. Direct students to use their Writing Form to respond to their prompt.

Visual Literacy

Writing Form

The Sun and Stars

Although stars seem mysterious, they are objects made of matter, just like everything else in the universe. Astronomers use telescopes to see clear images of stars and star clusters. A cluster of stars indicates a galaxy, or a group of stars that are pulled towards each other due to gravity.

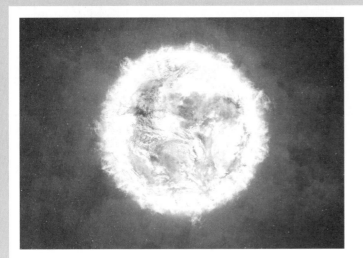

Scientists use telescopes and a star's appearance to infer as much information as they can about stars and galaxies. Stars vary in color, size, age, and luminosity. This photo shows the sun.

The Hubble Space Telescope has been orbiting Earth since 1990 and has captured hundreds of thousands of images from deep space. It works by capturing light released from objects in space such as stars. Before Hubble, astronomers used telescopes on Earth's surface, but the Earth's atmosphere prevented the images from being as clear as possible.

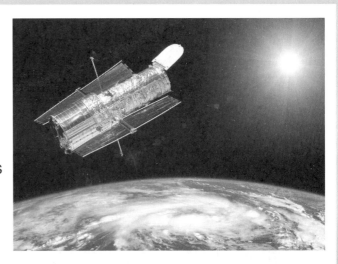

Name _____

The Sun and Stars

_____

_____

_____

_____

_____

_____

_____

_____

_____

_____

_____

_____

_____

_____

_____

_____

_____

_____

Writing Form

Nonfiction Reading Practice • EMC 3235 • © Evan-Moor Corp.

Words to Know	**Words to Know**	**Words to Know**
What Are Stars?	**Look at the Stars**	**Stars and Us**

sphere	astronomers	astronomers
hydrogen	luminosity	helium
helium	clusters	hydrogen
electromagnetic radiation	orbiting	luminosity
Milky Way	Hubble Space Telescope	light-years
galaxy	pinpoints	circumference
	galaxies	Hubble Space Telescope
	moderately	obtained
	interstellar matter	positioned
	obstructing	atmosphere
		capture
		interstellar

The Sun and Stars ■   The Sun and Stars ■ ■   The Sun and Stars ■ ■ ■

What Are Stars?

It's a clear summer night, and you look up at the sky. There are bright, twinkling objects floating in the darkness. They look like little diamonds, but, of course, they're stars. Some look bigger, and some look brighter. But why do they look different?

What is a star?

A star is a massive glowing sphere of burning hot gases. It is mostly made up of hydrogen and helium, but there are other gases, too. Stars produce lots of energy that flows out and into space.

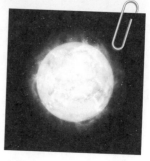

What kind of energy do stars produce?

Stars produce electromagnetic radiation, which is all around us. Electromagnetic radiation comes in different forms, shown in the diagram below. It can be radiant and visible (visible light is an example), or it can be invisible (such as radio waves). A twinkling star is continuously releasing this radiation. When we see a star shining in the sky, we are actually seeing visible light.

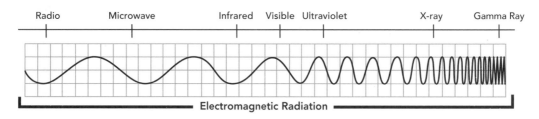

Radio Microwave Infrared Visible Ultraviolet X-ray Gamma Ray

Electromagnetic Radiation

What is the sun?

The sun is a star, similar to billions of other stars in the Milky Way. It produces great amounts of electromagnetic radiation, which is why people wear sun protection even though Earth is over 92 million miles (150 million km) away. Scientists estimate that it is about 4.6 billion years old. It is made up of mostly hydrogen and helium gases. The sun burns so hot that the temperature of its core is believed to be 27 million degrees Fahrenheit (15 million degrees Celsius). The sun is so large that scientists believe it could fit about one million Earths inside it. It's no wonder that our sun looks like the brightest star in the sky!

Why do other stars look smaller than the sun?

Other stars in the galaxy look smaller than the sun in our solar system because of their distance from Earth. The sun is the closest star to us. When we look up at the starry night sky, it is not immediately apparent that all of the stars differ in distance from us and from each other. Sometimes it seems as though stars are close to each other when they are actually trillions of miles/kilometers apart.

What Are Stars?

Fill in the circle by the correct answer. Then write the answers to numbers 3, 4, and 5.

1. According to the text, stars _____.
   Ⓐ range in size and in distance from Earth
   Ⓑ are all the same distance from Earth
   Ⓒ are all the same size and temperature
   Ⓓ can be seen only with a telescope

2. The diagram shows that electromagnetic radiation _____.
   Ⓐ is everywhere we go
   Ⓑ is always visible
   Ⓒ moves in a straight line
   Ⓓ moves in waves

3. Explain what the sun is composed of.

   _____

   _____

4. What effect does the distance from Earth have on how stars appear to us?

   _____

   _____

5. Explain which forms of electromagnetic radiation you are familiar with and how.

   _____

   _____

Write About the Topic

Use the Writing Form to write about what you read.

Compare and contrast the sun in our solar system to the other stars in the galaxy. Use details and examples from the text.

Look at the Stars

Stars are massive glowing balls of fire and gas. Not all stars are alike, and some stand out more than others. Astronomers can determine a star's approximate distance from Earth, luminosity, temperature, and color.

A Star's Distance from Earth

Everybody sees the stars from the same viewpoint: Earth. Stars are very far away from Earth. We can't simply jump on a spaceship and travel millions of miles/kilometers into space to get a closer look. The closest star to Earth, our sun, is over 92 million miles (150 million km) away. It is the only star in our solar system. Because stars are so distant, astronomers use measurements and other clues to determine which stars are closer or farther away. Stars that are closer to Earth appear bigger and brighter.

A Star's Luminosity

Luminosity is a star's brightness. Astronomers calculate luminosity by measuring how much energy a star releases. Stars that release more energy in the visible range are brighter. Larger stars produce more energy because they have a larger core, which results in more energy flowing out. The energy is in the form of heat and light. A lot of the energy flows into outer space and stays there, but some travels to planets such as Earth. As a star ages, it becomes hotter and brighter.

Star clusters are very bright and can indicate that a group of stars are orbiting around each other. The Hubble Space Telescope, a telescope that orbits Earth, has picked up pinpoints of bright light in the farthest, darkest parts of the universe. Some astronomers believe that these pinpoints are entire galaxies, each containing millions of stars.

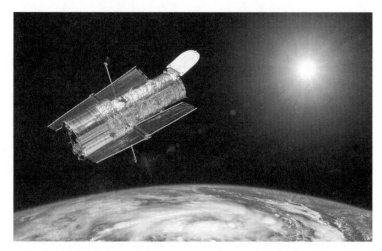

The Hubble Space Telescope was launched into space in 1990. It captures some space images that ordinary telescopes on Earth's surface can't access.

A Star's Temperature and Color

A star's heat affects its color. The coolest stars in the galaxy appear red. Stars that burn at a moderately hot level appear orange or yellow. The hottest stars look white or blue. Interstellar matter (objects, gases, and dust that float through space) can affect how we view luminosity and color by partly obstructing our view of a star. Interstellar matter can make stars appear redder and dimmer, for example. This could lead astronomers to believe that a star is farther away than it actually is.

Name _____

Look at the Stars

Fill in the circle by the correct answer. Then write the answers to numbers 3, 4, and 5.

1. The brightness of a star can indicate _____.
   - Ⓐ an entire galaxy
   - Ⓑ a star's age
   - Ⓒ which telescope is required
   - Ⓓ a star's name

2. The sun appears bigger and brighter than other stars partly because it's _____.
   - Ⓐ farthest from Earth
   - Ⓑ near our solar system
   - Ⓒ yellow
   - Ⓓ closest to Earth

3. Why do you think it's important for astronomers to study stars?

   _____

   _____

4. What inferences could you make about a small red star in the sky? Explain why.

   _____

   _____

5. Did the photo help you understand the text better? Explain why or why not.

   _____

   _____

Write About the Topic

Use the Writing Form to write about what you read.

Explain how a scientist could use a star's appearance to learn more about stars and galaxies. Use details and examples.

Stars and Us

Stars are beautiful, but they are not all the same. Astronomers use technology and images to learn more about stars, galaxies, and deep space.

Stars in Relation to Earth

Stars are massive glowing spheres of burning hot gases (mostly helium and hydrogen). They vary in brightness, or luminosity, size, color, age, and distance from Earth. The sun is the closest star to Earth, and it is over 92 million miles (150 million km) away. Because the distances between objects in space are so enormous, astronomers measure them in units of light-years. A single light-year is the distance light travels in one year. This is a tremendous distance, considering that light can travel around the entire circumference of Earth 7.5 times in one second.

Star Name	Light-Years/Kilometers from Earth
Proxima Centauri	4.2/40 trillion
Rigil Kentaurus	4.4/42 trillion
Barnard's Star	6.0/57 trillion

When we see stars, we are actually viewing light that was released from a star billions of years ago. The light has been traveling through space nonstop, and it has taken this long to get to us. We see what the stars looked like back then.

The Hubble Space Telescope Helps Us Look at Stars

The Hubble Space Telescope was launched into Earth's orbit in 1990. It has obtained clearer images in deep space than those from Earth-based telescopes. It's positioned above Earth's surface, so light in Earth's atmosphere doesn't interfere with images it picks up. This allows Hubble to capture more light from interstellar objects, create a clear and detailed image, and send it down to our computers. Hubble has obtained hundreds of thousands of space images.

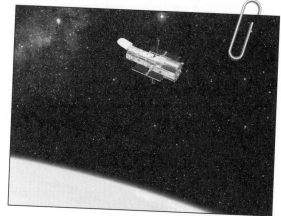

Hubble observes stars in deep space.

Stars Change Over Time

Newer stars are not as hot or as bright as older stars. Younger stars glow red and appear dimmer. Older stars look yellow. The oldest stars appear white or blue. Sometimes stars shrink or explode. The largest stars can remain for millions of years, the medium-sized stars can last for billions of years, and the smallest stars can burn for trillions of years. But all stars come to an end eventually.

   Nonfiction Reading Practice • EMC 3235 • © Evan-Moor Corp.

Stars and Us

Fill in the circle by the correct answer. Then write the answers to numbers 3, 4, and 5.

1. A star's appearance can _____.
   - Ⓐ indicate its age
   - Ⓑ indicate who discovered it
   - Ⓒ reveal its name
   - Ⓓ give clues about the telescope

2. Hubble depends on _____ to obtain clear deep-space images.
   - Ⓐ light in Earth's atmosphere
   - Ⓑ light released from interstellar objects
   - Ⓒ Proxima Centauri and Barnard's Star
   - Ⓓ darkness emanating from Earth's surface

3. Would you rather study a Hubble image than one from another telescope?
   Why or why not?

   _____

   _____

4. Explain why stars differ in appearance.

   _____

   _____

5. If you could invent one tool to study stars, what would it be, and what would it do?

   _____

   _____

Write About the Topic

Use the Writing Form to write about what you read.

Is it important for astronomers to study stars? Write an argument for why or why not. Use details from the text.

Extraordinary Food, Ordinary Math

Level 1 ■
Words to Know list, Reading Selection, and Reading Comprehension questions

Level 2 ■ ■
Words to Know list, Reading Selection, and Reading Comprehension questions

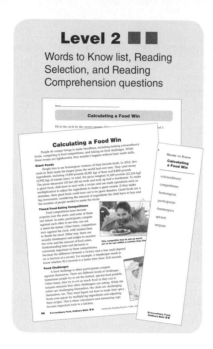

Level 3 ■ ■ ■
Words to Know list, Reading Selection, and Reading Comprehension questions

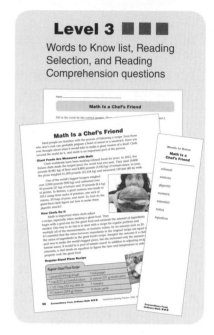

Assemble the Unit

Reproduce and distribute one copy for each student:

- Visual Literacy page: Extraordinary Food, Ordinary Math, page 91
- Level 1, 2, or 3 Reading Selection and Reading Comprehension page and the corresponding Words to Know list
- Graphic Organizer of your choosing, provided on pages 180–186
- Writing Form: Extraordinary Food, Ordinary Math, page 92

Introduce the Topic

Read aloud and discuss the Extraordinary Food, Ordinary Math photo and list. Explain that math is an essential part of enjoying giant foods and food challenges because it's math and measurements that make the food extraordinary.

Read and Respond

Form leveled groups and review the Words to Know lists with each group of students. Instruct each group to read their selection individually, in pairs, or as a group. Have students complete the Reading Comprehension page for their selection.

Write About the Topic

Read aloud the leveled writing prompt for each group. Tell students to use the Graphic Organizer to plan their writing. Direct students to use their Writing Form to respond to their prompt.

Visual Literacy

Writing Form

Extraordinary Food, Ordinary Math

People around the world love giant versions of their favorite foods. There have been giant sandwiches, giant pizzas, giant servings of mashed potatoes, giant lasagnas, and so much more.

How do the giant-food chefs figure out the process of making a humongous food? They probably do a number of things to accomplish the challenging task, and one thing that likely comes in handy is math.

People Use Math to Make Food

People...

- estimate how many ingredients are needed

- estimate the cost of ingredients

- increase the amount of ingredients to cook with

- use a ratio of ingredients that makes the giant food recognizable

- figure out how to cook the food

- figure out how long to cook the food

- weigh and measure the food

- compare the food's measurements to other foods' measurements

Name _____

Extraordinary Food, Ordinary Math

_____

_____

_____

_____

_____

_____

_____

_____

_____

_____

_____

_____

_____

_____

_____

_____

_____

_____

_____

_____

_____

Nonfiction Reading Practice • EMC 3235 • © Evan-Moor Corp.

Words to Know	Words to Know	Words to Know
Giant Snack, Giant Equation	**Calculating a Food Win**	**Math Is a Chef's Friend**
unique	extraordinary	colossal
gigantic	competitions	samosa
humongous	humongous	gigantic
trough	participants	numeric
operations	timekeepers	essential
resemble	spiciest	ratios
percentages	surpass	equation

Extraordinary Food, Ordinary Math ■

Extraordinary Food, Ordinary Math ■ ■

Extraordinary Food, Ordinary Math ■ ■ ■

Giant Snack, Giant Equation

People do unique things to set world records, and making gigantic foods is one of them. Making a humongous snack isn't only about cooking skills, it's also about math skills.

Giant Foods

What if you could have a gigantic serving of your favorite food? Well, pizza lovers in Italy got just that. In 2012, five Italian chefs made the largest pizza the world had ever seen. They used many ingredients, including 19,800 pounds (8,981 kg) of flour and 8,800 pounds (3,992 kg) of tomato sauce. In total, the pizza weighed 51,200 pounds (23,224 kg) and measured 130 feet (40 m) wide. The previous largest pizza was made in 1990 in South Africa and weighed 27,000 pounds (12,247 kg).

There have been other giant foods, including a giant meatball, peanut butter cup, and hot dog. One of the biggest burgers weighed over 2,000 pounds (900 kg) and contained over 50 pounds (27 kg) of lettuce. And a giant serving of nachos was once served in an 80-foot-long (24-meter-long) trough. It had 4,689 pounds (2,127 kg) of chips, cheese, and meat.

Using Math to Make Giant Foods

Imagine that some chefs are trying to make the largest pizza ever. First, they'd consider the size of the current largest pizza. Then, they'd use a normal-sized pizza recipe for reference. Suppose a 2-pound (0.9 kg) ball of dough can create a 20-inch (51-cm) crust. The chefs could use this information to multiply the measurements and estimate the amount of ingredients needed for the giant pizza. They could use math operations to determine how long to cook the giant pizza based on the cooking time for the original recipe.

Normal Pizza Recipe in Ounces/Grams	Giant Pizza Recipe in Ounces/Grams
15 oz. dough (425 g)	15,000 oz. dough (425,243 g)
9 oz. sauce (255 g)	9,000 oz. sauce (255,146 g)
12 oz. cheese (340 g)	12,000 oz. cheese (340,194 g)

One challenge would be creating even ratios of ingredients (tomato sauce, dough, cheese, and toppings) between the normal pizza's ingredients and the giant pizza's. For example, if a normal pizza's dough and sauce have a ratio of 5:3 as in the recipe above, then the ratio of dough and sauce in the giant pizza needs to be 5:3, as well. Otherwise, the giant result might not resemble pizza at all! The chefs would probably use fractions or percentages to determine how to divide the work and use addition to calculate the pizza's total weight.

Name _____

Giant Snack, Giant Equation

Fill in the circle by the correct answer. Then write the answers to numbers 3, 4, and 5.

1. Math is used in the area of giant foods to _____.
   Ⓐ measure and compare foods
   Ⓑ study a chef's skills
   Ⓒ use as much food as possible
   Ⓓ share food with the world

2. Details about the specific portions in a recipe _____.
   Ⓐ reveal when the giant food will expire
   Ⓑ aren't helpful for other chefs who want to make giant foods
   Ⓒ help us understand why the chefs chose to make this food
   Ⓓ would be useful for a chef trying to make a giant portion

3. How could the steps of making a giant pizza be applied to making other giant foods?

   _____

   _____

4. Which math operations do you think are most useful when making a giant food?

   _____

   _____

5. Are weight and measurement an important part of this text? Explain why or why not.

   _____

   _____

Write About the Topic

Use the Writing Form to write about what you read.

> Describe some of the possible outcomes if there wasn't an equal ratio of ingredients between the giant and normal pizzas.

© Evan-Moor Corp. • EMC 3235 • Nonfiction Reading Practice   **Extraordinary Food, Ordinary Math** ■   95

Calculating a Food Win

People do unique things to make headlines, including making extraordinary foods, competing in food competitions, and taking on food challenges. While these events are lighthearted, they wouldn't happen without basic math skills.

Giant Foods

People love to see humongous versions of their favorite foods. In 2012, five chefs in Italy made the largest pizza the world had ever seen. They used many ingredients, including 19,800 pounds (8,981 kg) of flour and 8,800 pounds (3,992 kg) of tomato sauce. In total, the pizza weighed 51,200 pounds (23,224 kg)! The pizza measured 130 feet (40 m) wide and took up half a warehouse. To make a giant food, chefs have to start with a recipe and use math operations such as multiplication to adjust the ingredients to make a giant version. If they make mistakes, their giant foods could turn out to be giant disasters. Giant foods are a big investment, considering the amount of ingredients the chefs have to buy and the number of people needed to make the foods.

Timed Food-Eating Competitions

Food competitions have become popular over the years, and some of them are timed. In some, participants compete against each other to see who can eat a meal the fastest. Other times, competitors race against the clock, with limited time to finish the meal. Either way, there are usually timekeepers and judges to monitor the time and the amount of food eaten. Understanding time and decimals is extremely important in these competitions,

This competitor has to eat as much pie as he can within a certain time limit.

because the difference between a victory and a loss could depend on a fraction of a second. For example, a timekeeper needs to know whether 30.2 seconds is a faster time than 30.8 seconds.

Food Challenges

A food challenge is when participants compete against themselves. There are different kinds of challenges. Sometimes people try to eat the hottest, spiciest food possible. Other times, they try to eat as much food as they can to surpass amounts that other challengers are eating. While the eaters are challenging themselves, the chefs are challenging themselves, too. They must figure out how to make their spicy foods even spicier by multiplying ingredients and adjusting their recipes. This is when calculators and measuring cups become important tools in a kitchen.

Name _____

Calculating a Food Win

Fill in the circle by the correct answer. Then write the answers to numbers 3, 4, and 5.

1. The chefs of giant foods and food challenges probably use math to _____.
   - Ⓐ taste their food as they are cooking it
   - Ⓑ adjust recipes to make foods larger or hotter
   - Ⓒ receive attention for setting a new world record
   - Ⓓ adjust their uniforms for the difficult task

2. Mark the food-eating competitor's time that is the fastest.
   - Ⓐ 2.04
   - Ⓑ 2.07
   - Ⓒ 2.47
   - Ⓓ 2.49

3. List anything related to math that a chef would do when making the largest pizza ever.

   _____

   _____

4. How could math skills help a competitive eater in a timed competition?

   _____

   _____

5. Explain the steps a chef could take to figure out how much it costs to make a giant food.

   _____

   _____

Write About the Topic
Use the Writing Form to write about what you read.

> Would food competitions and food records be possible without using math? Write an argument explaining why or why not.

Math Is a Chef's Friend

Most people are familiar with the process of following a recipe. Even those who don't cook can probably prepare a bowl of cereal or a sandwich. Have you ever thought about what it would take to make a giant version of a food? Chefs around the world do it, and math is an important part of the process.

Giant Foods Are Measured with Math

Chefs worldwide have been making colossal foods for years. In 2012, five Italian chefs made the largest pizza the world had ever seen. They used 19,800 pounds (8,981 kg) of flour and 8,800 pounds (3,992 kg) of tomato sauce. In total, the pizza weighed 51,200 pounds (23,224 kg) and measured 130 feet (40 m) wide.

One of the world's biggest burgers weighed over 2,000 pounds (900 kg) and contained over 50 pounds (27 kg) of lettuce and 19 pounds (8.6 kg) of pickles. In Britain, a giant samosa was made in 2012 using three sacks of potatoes, one sack of onions, 30 bags of peas, and more. So, how do the giant-food chefs figure out how to make these gigantic snacks?

How Chefs Do It

Math is important when chefs adjust a recipe, especially when making a giant food. They begin with a goal-size for the giant food and estimate the amount of ingredients needed. One way to do this is to start with a recipe for regular portions and multiply all of the measurements, or numeric values, by an amount such as 20. It's essential that the ratios between ingredients in the original recipe are equal to the ratios of ingredients in the giant food's recipe. Imagine the outcome if a chef's goal was to make the world's biggest pizza, but she increased only the amount of tomato sauce. It would be a pool of tomato sauce! In addition to adjusting recipe amounts, a chef needs an equation to figure the time and temperature in order to properly cook the giant food.

Regular-Sized Pizza Recipe

Regular-Sized Pizza Recipe	
1 pound (0.45 kg) dough	1 bell pepper
1 cup (237 g) tomato sauce	2 ounces (57 g) mushrooms
1 1/2 Tbsp. (22 mL) olive oil	1 tomato
10 ounces (283 g) cheese	2 cloves garlic

Name _____

Math Is a Chef's Friend

Fill in the circle by the correct answer. Then write the answers to numbers 3, 4, and 5.

1. Math is important in the area of giant foods because _____.
   Ⓐ people enjoy using a lot of ingredients
   Ⓑ the flavors of giant foods can be measured
   Ⓒ it is used to measure and compare ratios of ingredients
   Ⓓ it helps determine which ingredients are needed

2. Math is helpful in adjusting recipes because _____.
   Ⓐ there are so many ingredients in all recipes
   Ⓑ most people don't use recipes or measurements
   Ⓒ it's not necessary to use accurate ingredients in most recipes
   Ⓓ recipes have measurements that can be multiplied

3. Explain why ratios are important when chefs adjust recipes or make giant foods.

   _____

   _____

4. Could you apply the information in the text if you were trying to make a smaller version of a food? Explain why or why not.

   _____

   _____

5. Do you agree with the title "Math Is a Chef's Friend"? Explain your answer.

   _____

   _____

Write About the Topic

Use the Writing Form to write about what you read.

> Think of a food you can make. Explain the steps and the math operations you would use to make it for one hundred people.

A Business Uses Math

Level 1 ■
Words to Know list, Reading Selection, and Reading Comprehension questions

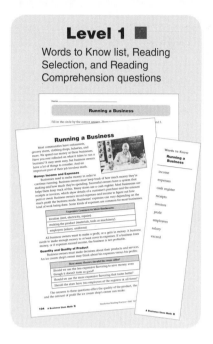

Level 2 ■ ■
Words to Know list, Reading Selection, and Reading Comprehension questions

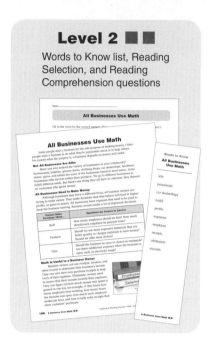

Level 3 ■ ■ ■
Words to Know list, Reading Selection, and Reading Comprehension questions

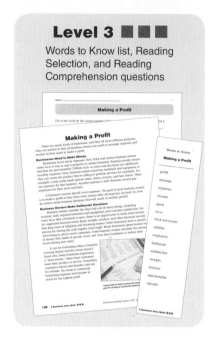

Assemble the Unit
Reproduce and distribute one copy for each student:

- Visual Literacy page: A Business Uses Math, page 101
- Level 1, 2, or 3 Reading Selection and Reading Comprehension page and the corresponding Words to Know list
- Graphic Organizer of your choosing, provided on pages 180–186
- Writing Form: A Business Uses Math, page 102

Visual Literacy

Introduce the Topic
Read aloud the text and discuss the photos on page 101. Point out that there are many kinds of businesses, and ask students what kinds of businesses they have visited. Explain that all businesses depend on money, and they need to make enough money to cover their expenses. Point out that math is useful to business owners.

Read and Respond
Form leveled groups and review the Words to Know lists with each group of students. Instruct each group to read their selection individually, in pairs, or as a group. Have students complete the Reading Comprehension page for their selection.

Writing Form

Write About the Topic
Read aloud the leveled writing prompt for each group. Tell students to use the Graphic Organizer to plan their writing. Direct students to use their Writing Form to respond to their prompt.

A Business Uses Math

Communities have many different kinds of businesses that fulfill various needs. Although it might seem like no two businesses are alike, they do have one thing in common: they depend on paying customers.

Math is useful to business owners. It's extremely important for a business to keep track of its expenses and its income in order to determine if it's making a profit. A business is unsuccessful if the total amount of its expenses exceeds its total income.

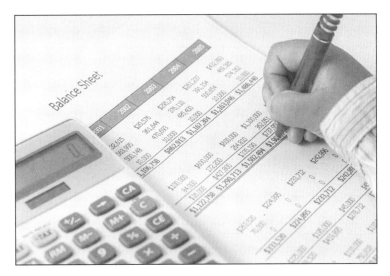

Successful business: **Expenses** $<$ **Income**

Name _____

A Business Uses Math

_____
_____
_____
_____
_____
_____
_____
_____
_____
_____
_____
_____
_____
_____
_____
_____
_____
_____
_____
_____
_____

Nonfiction Reading Practice • EMC 3235 • © Evan-Moor Corp.

Words to Know	Words to Know	Words to Know
Running a Business	**All Businesses Use Math**	**Making a Profit**
income	sole	profit
expenses	passionate	manage
cash register	car dealerships	expenses
receipts	fulfill	income
invoices	profits	quest
profit	expenses	incur
employees	employee	brick and mortar
salary	receipts	utilities
exceed	ultimately	employees
	exceeds	deliberate
		satisfaction
		receipts
		invoices
		merchandise
		refunds

Running a Business

Most communities have restaurants, grocery stores, clothing shops, bakeries, and more. We spend our money at these businesses. Have you ever reflected on what it takes to run a business? It may seem easy, but business owners have a lot of things to consider. And an important part of their job involves math.

Money: Income and Expenses

Businesses need to make money in order to continue running. Business owners must keep track of how much money they're making and how much they're spending. Successful owners have a system that helps them keep track of this. Many stores use a cash register. Most businesses use receipts or invoices, which show details of a customer's purchase and the amount paid or owed. Business owners record expenses and income to figure out how much profit the business made. Businesses' expenses can vary depending on the kind of work being done. Some kinds of expenses are common for most businesses.

Expenses Common to Most Businesses:
location (rent, electricity, repairs)
making the product (materials, tools or machinery)
employees (salary, uniforms)

All business owners want to make a profit, or a gain in money. A business needs to make enough money to at least cover its expenses. If a business loses money, or if expenses exceed income, the business is not profitable.

Quantity and Quality of Product

Business owners must make decisions about their products and services. An ice cream shop's owner may think about his expenses versus his profits:

How many flavors should the store offer?
Should we use the less expensive flavoring to save money, even though it doesn't taste as good?
Should we use the more expensive flavoring that tastes better?
Should the store have two employees at the registers at all times?

The answers to these questions affect the quality of the product, the service, and the amount of profit the ice cream shop's owner can make.

  Nonfiction Reading Practice • EMC 3235 • © Evan-Moor Corp.

Running a Business

Fill in the circle by the correct answer. Then write the answers to numbers 3, 4, and 5.

1. Business owners can use receipts to _____.
   - Ⓐ calculate total purchases
   - Ⓑ improve how the cash register functions
   - Ⓒ provide a service to a customer
   - Ⓓ create a product to sell

2. Math is useful to business owners because it _____.
   - Ⓐ is the most important school subject
   - Ⓑ teaches them how to be patient with customers
   - Ⓒ helps them make decisions that lead to a bigger profit
   - Ⓓ helps them attract more customers

3. Explain how a business owner can determine whether or not a profit is being made.

   _____

   _____

4. Name a business in your town. Then write a question the owner may have considered.

   _____

   _____

5. List two ways in which an ice cream shop is similar to a sock shop.

   _____

   _____

Write About the Topic

Use the Writing Form to write about what you read.

Explain what would happen if a business owner didn't consider income and expenses. Use text details and your own examples.

All Businesses Use Math

Some people start a business for the sole purpose of making money. Other people start a business to do what they're passionate about or to help others. No matter what the purpose is, a business depends on money and math.

Not All Businesses Are Alike

Have you ever noticed the variety of businesses in your community? Restaurants, bakeries, grocery stores, clothing shops, car dealerships, hardware stores, gyms, and salons are some of the businesses found in most towns. Some businesses offer services rather than products. We go to different businesses to fulfill different needs. But there's one thing they all have in common: they depend on customers who spend money.

All Businesses Need to Make Money

Although businesses may have a different focus, all business owners are trying to make money. They make decisions that they believe will lead to higher profits, or gains in money. All businesses have expenses that need to be paid to keep the business running. Business owners make a lot of important decisions.

Owners Make Decisions About...	Questions for Owners to Answer
Staff	How many employees should we hire? How much should each employee be paid per hour?
Products	Should we use more expensive materials that are better quality or cheaper materials to save money? Should we offer more choices?
Time	Should the business be open or closed on weekends? Are there additional expenses when the business is open, such as electricity usage?

Math Is Useful to a Business Owner

Business owners can use receipts, invoices, and other records to determine their business's income. They can save their own purchase receipts to keep track of their expenses. Ultimately, owners need to ensure that their income exceeds their expenses. They can figure out how much money was spent or gained in one day, for example, if they know how many employees were working, how many hours the business was open, how much each employee makes per hour, and how to tally sales receipts that show customers' purchases.

Nonfiction Reading Practice • EMC 3235 • © Evan-Moor Corp.

Name _____

All Businesses Use Math

Fill in the circle by the correct answer. Then write the answers to numbers 3, 4, and 5.

1. Which is a similarity between a restaurant and a bookstore?
   - Ⓐ Its main expense has an expiration date.
   - Ⓑ The business uses equipment to make its products.
   - Ⓒ Customers purchase a product they can use for years.
   - Ⓓ Customers pay to receive a product.

2. Business owners could _____ if they notice that their expenses exceed their income.
   - Ⓐ change their purpose
   - Ⓑ cut expenses by using cheaper materials
   - Ⓒ hire more staff and give them a raise in pay
   - Ⓓ change the store's hours to a time that's less busy

3. Describe some math operations a business owner could use to calculate a day's income.

   _____

   _____

4. Why would owners choose to keep a business open for fewer hours?

   _____

   _____

5. Why are profits significant for a business?

   _____

   _____

Write About the Topic

Use the Writing Form to write about what you read.

> Do math and money affect every decision a business owner makes? Write an argument for why or why not. Use text details.

Making a Profit

There are many kinds of businesses, and they all serve different purposes. They are similar in that all business owners use math to manage expenses and income in their quest to make a profit.

Businesses Need to Make Money

Businesses incur many expenses. First, brick and mortar business owners either have to buy or rent a property to conduct business. Renting usually means that fees are paid monthly. Utilities such as water and electricity are additional monthly expenses. Next, business owners must buy materials and equipment so they can create the product they're selling or perform services for customers. For example, a hair salon needs special sinks, chairs, scissors, and hair dryers. These are expenses for that business. Another expense is staff. Business owners pay employees for their work and time.

A business's income should cover expenses. The goal of most business owners is to make a profit so they have extra money after all expenses are paid. So, how do owners make business decisions that will result in healthy profits?

Business Owners Make Deliberate Decisions

Business owners consider the time and cost of many things, including location, staff, required materials and equipment, and customer satisfaction. For every hour that a business is open, there is an opportunity to make more money. An organized business owner keeps receipts, invoices, and other financial records that keep track of outgoing and incoming money. Some businesses have a specific process for closing the cash register every night. Many businesses spend money on advertising to attract more customers. Some business owners calculate the amount of money they make at specific times and close their businesses or reduce their hours during slow times.

It can be frustrating when a business is losing money and the owner doesn't know why. Some businesses experience a "slow season," when fewer customers want their product or service. Sometimes, customers return merchandise and ask for refunds. An owner is constantly balancing expenses and income to reach for the highest profit.

Using math to total income and expenses is part of running a successful business.

Nonfiction Reading Practice • EMC 3235 • © Evan-Moor Corp.

Making a Profit

Fill in the circle by the correct answer. Then write the answers to numbers 3, 4, and 5.

1. Business owners who calculate their business's average weekly income _____.
   Ⓐ must have a successful business
   Ⓑ probably make business decisions without considering records
   Ⓒ cannot estimate how much their expenses will be per week
   Ⓓ can estimate how much money the business makes in a year

2. A business is not profitable if _____.
   Ⓐ the expenses are covered by the income
   Ⓑ the owner has too few staff members
   Ⓒ its expenses exceed its income
   Ⓓ its income exceeds its expenses

3. Explain how math plays a role in a business owner's decision making.

   _____

   _____

4. Why is time an important consideration for business owners?

   _____

   _____

5. Could a business owner be successful without financial records? Explain your answer.

   _____

   _____

Write About the Topic

Use the Writing Form to write about what you read.

Describe an idea for your own business. Tell what its purpose is and other details. Explain how you'd use math to make a profit.

Video Game Development

Level 1 ■
Words to Know list, Reading Selection, and Reading Comprehension questions

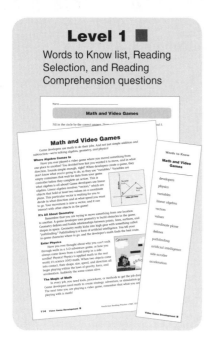

Level 2 ■ ■
Words to Know list, Reading Selection, and Reading Comprehension questions

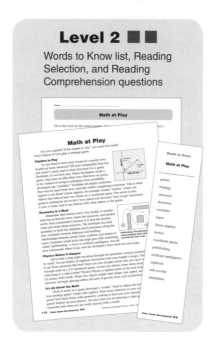

Level 3 ■ ■ ■
Words to Know list, Reading Selection, and Reading Comprehension questions

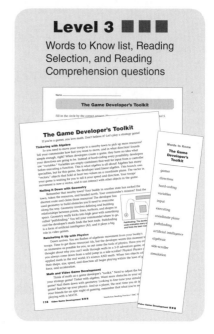

Assemble the Unit

Reproduce and distribute one copy for each student:

- Visual Literacy page: Video Game Development, page 111
- Level 1, 2, or 3 Reading Selection and Reading Comprehension page and the corresponding Words to Know list
- Graphic Organizer of your choosing, provided on pages 180–186
- Writing Form: Video Game Development, page 112

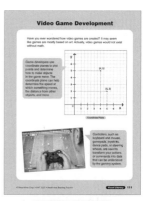

Visual Literacy

Introduce the Topic

Read aloud and discuss the Video Game Development text and graphics. Explain that the one thing that all video games have in common is math and movement. Video games are based on images moving on the screen; the images are controlled by a player's game controller. Math is required to make that possible.

Read and Respond

Form leveled groups and review the Words to Know lists with each group of students. Instruct each group to read their selection individually, in pairs, or as a group. Have students complete the Reading Comprehension page for their selection.

Writing Form

Write About the Topic

Read aloud the leveled writing prompt for each group. Tell students to use the Graphic Organizer to plan their writing. Direct students to use their Writing Form to respond to their prompt.

Nonfiction Reading Practice • EMC 3235 • © Evan-Moor Corp.

Video Game Development

Have you ever wondered how video games are created? It may seem like games are mostly based on art. Actually, video games would not exist without math.

Game developers use coordinate planes to plot points and determine how to make objects in the game move. The coordinate plane can help determine the speed at which something moves, the distance from other objects, and more.

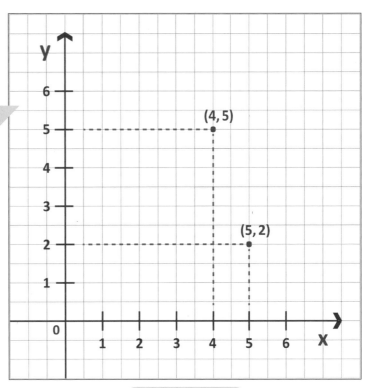

Coordinate Plane

Controllers, such as keyboard and mouse, gamepads, joysticks, dance pads, or steering wheels, are used to transform your actions or commands into data that can be understood by the gaming system.

Name _____

Video Game Development

_____

_____

_____

_____

_____

_____

_____

_____

_____

_____

_____

_____

_____

_____

_____

_____

_____

_____

_____

Words to Know	Words to Know	Words to Know
Math and Video Games	**Math at Play**	**The Game Developer's Toolkit**
developers	gamer	gamer
physics	strategy	directives
variables	resources	hard-coding
linear algebra	directives	variables
vectors	variables	input
values	input	executing
coordinate plane	linear algebra	coordinate plane
defines	vectors	pathfinding
pathfinding	coordinate plane	artificial intelligence
artificial intelligence	pathfinding	algebraic
side-scroller	artificial intelligence	side-scroller
acceleration	algebraic	simulation
	side-scroller	
	simulation	
Video Game Development ■	**Video Game Development** ■ ■	**Video Game Development** ■ ■ ■

Math and Video Games

Game developers use math to do their jobs. And not just simple addition and subtraction—we're talking algebra, geometry, and physics!

Where Algebra Comes In

Have you ever played a video game where you moved something from one place to another? You decided how fast you wanted it to move, and in what direction. Sounds simple enough, right? When developers create a game, they don't know what you're going to do, so they use "variables." Variables are empty containers that wait for data from your game controller before they complete an action. This is what algebra is all about! Game developers use linear algebra. Linear algebra involves "vectors," which are objects that hold at least two values on a coordinate plane. This particular vector is waiting for you to decide in what direction and at what speed you want to go. Your movement is now a vector, and it can interact with other objects in the game!

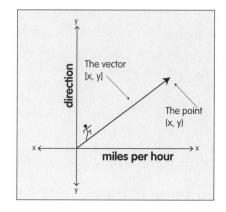

It's All About Geometry

Remember that you are trying to move something from one location to another. A game developer uses geometry to build obstacles in the game. Geometry defines and builds relationships between points, lines, surfaces, and shapes in space. Geometry really kicks into high gear with something called "pathfinding." Pathfinding is a form of artificial intelligence. You tell your in-game character where to go, and the developer's math finds the best route.

Enter Physics

Have you ever thought about why you can't walk through walls in a 3-D adventure game, or how you always come down from a solid jump in a side-scroller? Physics! Physics is applied math in the real world; it's science AND math. When two objects come into contact, their shape, size, speed, and direction all begin playing within the laws of gravity, force, and acceleration. Suddenly the scene comes alive.

The Magic of Math

In every job, you need tools, procedures, or methods to get the job done. Game developers need math to create strategy, adventure, or simulation games. The next time you are playing a video game, remember that what you are really playing with is math!

Name _____

Math and Video Games

Fill in the circle by the correct answer. Then write the answers to numbers 3, 4, and 5.

1. Video game developers use variables _____.
   Ⓐ to receive data
   Ⓑ to operate a game controller
   Ⓒ to hold values on a coordinate plane
   Ⓓ to apply geometry

2. The main idea of this text is that math _____.
   Ⓐ has nothing to do with art in video games
   Ⓑ doesn't affect video game players
   Ⓒ is helpful but not necessary in creating a video game
   Ⓓ is essential in creating a video game

3. Describe a video game you are familiar with and how geometry is used.

   _____

   _____

4. How does physics affect your game play?

   _____

   _____

5. Based on the text, what inference can you make about video game developers?

   _____

   _____

Write About the Topic

Use the Writing Form to write about what you read.

> Compare and contrast how you use math skills at school with how a game developer uses math skills.

Math at Play

Are you a gamer? If the answer is "yes," you must love math! Don't believe it? Let's play a strategy game.

Algebra in Play

So you need to move your troops to a nearby town to pick up more resources? Tell your commander how fast you want to move, and in what direction! For a game developer, it's not that easy. When developers create a game, they have no idea what your directives are going to be. Instead of trying to anticipate every possibility, developers use "variables." Variables are empty containers that wait for input from your controller before completing a function. This is what algebra is all about! Linear algebra, for example, studies "vectors," which are objects that hold at least two values on a coordinate plane. The vector in this game is waiting for you to tell it your speed and direction. Your troops' movement is now a vector, and it can interact with other objects in the game.

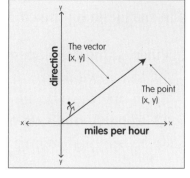

Geometry Is a Must

Remember that nearby town? Your buddy in another state has sacked the town, taken the resources, and headed north. Your commander's mission is to find the shortest route and claim those resources. The developer has used geometry to build the obstacles you'll encounter along the way. Geometry involves defining and building relationships between points, lines, surfaces, and shapes in space. Geometry really kicks into high gear with something called "pathfinding," a form of artificial intelligence. You tell your commander where to go, and the developer's math finds the best route.

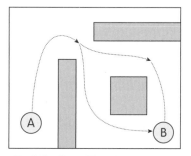

Pathfinding: The developer's code evaluates every option and finds the best route.

Physics Makes It Happen

You've had a long night traveling through the geometric canyons painted by math. You see flashes of algebraic movement from your buddy's troops. Time to get those resources! But how? Have you ever thought about why you can't walk through walls in a 3-D adventure game, or how you always come down from a solid jump in a side-scroller? Physics! Physics is applied math in the real world; it's science AND math. When two objects collide, their shape, size, speed, and direction all begin playing within the laws of gravity, force, and acceleration.

It's All About the Math

Think of math as a game developer's "toolkit." Need to adjust the balance in your strategy game? Tinker with algebra. Want more obstacles in your adventure game? Nail them down with geometry. Looking to fine-tune your simulation game? Ratchet up your physics. The next time you are playing a video game, remember that what you are really playing with is math!

   Nonfiction Reading Practice • EMC 3235 • © Evan-Moor Corp.

Name _____

Math at Play

Fill in the circle by the correct answer. Then write the answers to numbers 3, 4, and 5.

1. Video game developers use variables _____.
   - Ⓐ to make a coordinate plane
   - Ⓑ to follow the laws of physics
   - Ⓒ instead of trying to anticipate every possibility
   - Ⓓ to interact with objects in a game

2. We see physics as applied math in the real world when we _____.
   - Ⓐ see obstacles in a game
   - Ⓑ run into something
   - Ⓒ see how colorful a game environment is
   - Ⓓ choose a character to play the game as or with

3. Describe a video game you are familiar with and how geometry is used.

   _____

   _____

4. What is the main idea of this text?

   _____

   _____

5. Could a video game be created without using math? Explain why or why not.

   _____

   _____

Write About the Topic

Use the Writing Form to write about what you read.

Describe what a video game would be like if the developer used inaccurate math. Use your own examples and text details.

The Game Developer's Toolkit

If you're a gamer, you love math. Don't believe it? Let's play a strategy game!

Tinkering with Algebra

So you need to move your troops to a nearby town to pick up more resources? Tell your commander how fast you want to move, and in what direction! Sounds simple enough, right? When developers create a game, they have no idea what your directives are going to be. Instead of hard-coding every possibility, developers use "variables." Variables are empty containers that wait for input from a controller before executing a function. This is what algebra is all about! Algebra has many specialties, but for this game, the developer used linear algebra. This branch uses "vectors," objects that hold at least two values on a coordinate plane. The vector in your game is waiting for you to tell it your speed and direction. Your troops' movement is now a vector, and it can interact with other objects in the game.

Nailing It Down with Geometry

Remember that nearby town? Your buddy in another state has sacked the town, taken the resources, and headed north. Your commander's mission? Find the shortest route and claim those resources! The developer has used geometry to build obstacles you'll need to overcome along the way. Geometry involves defining and building relationships between points, lines, surfaces, and shapes in space. Geometry really kicks into high gear with something called "pathfinding." You tell your commander where to go, and the developer's math finds the best route. Pathfinding is a form of artificial intelligence (AI), and it plays a big role in video games.

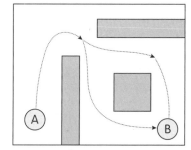

Pathfinding: The developer's code evaluates every option and finds the best route.

Ratcheting It Up with Physics

Dawn arrives. You see flashes of algebraic movement from your buddy's troops. Time to get those resources! Ah, but the developer wants this moment to be as immersive as possible for you, so out come the tools of physics. Have you ever thought about why you can't walk through walls in a 3-D adventure game, or how you always come down from a solid jump in a side-scroller? Physics! Physics is applied math in the real world; it's science AND math. When two objects collide, their shape, size, speed, and direction all begin playing within the laws of gravity, force, and acceleration.

Math and Video Game Development

Think of math as a game developer's "toolkit." Need to adjust the balance in your strategy game? Tinker with algebra. Want more obstacles in your adventure game? Nail them down with geometry. Looking to fine-tune your simulation game? Ratchet up your physics. And as a player, the next time you sit down with your friends for an epic night of gaming, remember that what you're really playing with is MATH.

The Game Developer's Toolkit

Fill in the circle by the correct answer. Then write the answers to numbers 3, 4, and 5.

1. Developers use variables _____.
   Ⓐ to establish directives
   Ⓑ to execute a function
   Ⓒ to hard-code every possibility
   Ⓓ to hold values

2. A game developer can use geometry to _____.
   Ⓐ plot a character's location on a coordinate plane
   Ⓑ create a vector
   Ⓒ create obstacles in the game
   Ⓓ define a variable

3. What would happen if a video game did not use vectors?

   _____

   _____

4. In your own words, explain pathfinding.

   _____

   _____

5. Explain why physics is important in a video game.

   _____

   _____

   _____

Write About the Topic

Use the Writing Form to write about what you read.

Explain how a game developer uses math to create a video game. Use details from the text.

The Field of Prosthetics

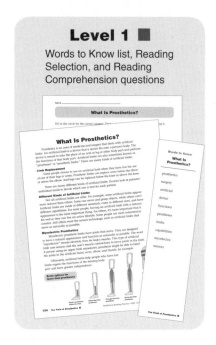
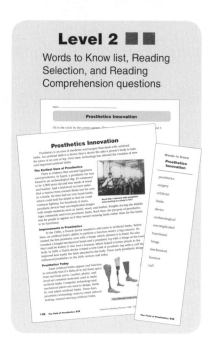
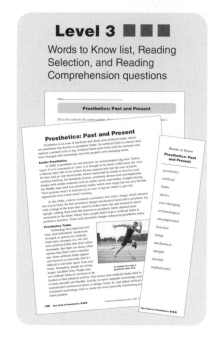
Assemble the Unit

Reproduce and distribute one copy for each student:

- Visual Literacy page: The Field of Prosthetics, page 121
- Level 1, 2, or 3 Reading Selection and Reading Comprehension page and the corresponding Words to Know list
- Graphic Organizer of your choosing, provided on pages 180–186
- Writing Form: The Field of Prosthetics, page 122

Introduce the Topic

Read aloud and discuss The Field of Prosthetics paragraphs and photos. Explain that some people choose to have a prosthetic limb to replace a lost or injured limb on their body. Point out that today, there are many options for artificial limbs because of advancements in technology.

Read and Respond

Form leveled groups and review the Words to Know lists with each group of students. Instruct each group to read their selection individually, in pairs, or as a group. Have students complete the Reading Comprehension page for their selection.

Write About the Topic

Read aloud the leveled writing prompt for each group. Tell students to use the Graphic Organizer to plan their writing. Direct students to use their Writing Form to respond to their prompt.

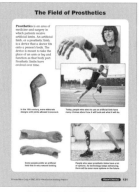

Visual Literacy

Writing Form

The Field of Prosthetics

Prosthetics is an area of medicine and surgery in which patients receive artificial limbs. An artificial limb, or a prosthetic limb, is a device that a doctor fits onto a person's body. The device is meant to take the place of an arm or leg and function as that body part. Prosthetic limbs have evolved over time.

In the 16th century, more elaborate designs with joints allowed movement.

Today, people who elect to use an artificial limb have many choices about how it will look and what it will do.

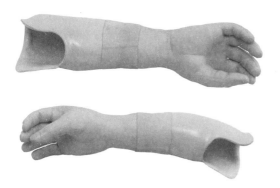

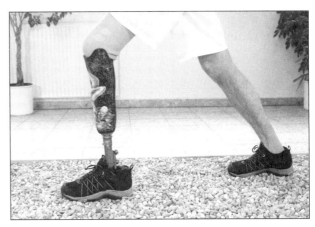

Some people prefer an artificial limb that is very natural looking.

People who wear prosthetic limbs have a lot of options. As technology keeps advancing, there will be even more options in the future.

Name _____

The Field of Prosthetics

_____

_____

_____

_____

_____

_____

_____

_____

_____

_____

_____

_____

_____

_____

_____

_____

_____

_____

_____

Words to Know	Words to Know	Words to Know
What Is Prosthetics?	**Prosthetics Innovation**	**Prosthetics: Past and Present**
prosthetics	prosthetics	prosthetics
surgery	surgery	artificial
artificial	artificial	limbs
device	limbs	device
functions	device	ever-changing
prostheses	archaeological	archaeological
limbs	uncomplicated	uncomplicated
capabilities	functional	function
myoelectric	hinge	hinge
sensors	mechanical	mechanical
	harness	upright
	cuff	durable
		sophisticated

The Field of Prosthetics ■   **The Field of Prosthetics** ■ ■   **The Field of Prosthetics** ■ ■ ■

What Is Prosthetics?

Prosthetics is an area of medicine and surgery that deals with artificial limbs. An artificial limb is a device that a doctor fits onto a person's body. The device is meant to take the place of an arm or leg or other body part and perform the functions of that body part. Artificial limbs are also sometimes known as "prostheses" or "prosthetic limbs." There are many kinds of artificial limbs.

Limb Replacement

Some people choose to use an artificial limb when they have lost the use of one of their legs or arms. Prosthetic limbs can replace arms below the elbow or above the elbow. And legs can be replaced below the knee or above the knee.

There are many different kinds of artificial limbs. Doctors look at patients' individual needs to decide which one is best for each patient.

Different Kinds of Artificial Limbs

Not all artificial limbs are alike. For example, some artificial limbs appear more natural than others. Some can move and grasp objects, while others can't. Artificial limbs are made of different materials, come in different sizes, and have different capabilities. For some people, having an artificial limb with a natural appearance is the most important thing. For others, it's more important that it fits well so they can live an active lifestyle. Some people are more interested in comfort. Still others want the newest technology, such as artificial limbs that move as naturally as possible.

Myoelectric Prosthetics

Myoelectric prosthetic limbs have joints that move. They are designed to have a natural appearance and function as naturally as possible. The word "myoelectric" means *electricity from the body's muscles*. This type of artificial limb uses sensors and the user's muscle contractions to move joints in the limb. A person using an upper limb myoelectric prosthesis might be able to bend the joints in the artificial hand, wrist, elbow, and thumb, for example.

Ultimately, artificial limbs help people who have lost limbs regain the functions of the missing body part and have greater independence.

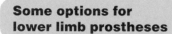

Some options for lower limb prostheses

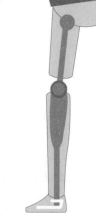

| Syme's prosthesis below the knee | Below-the-knee prosthesis | Through-the-knee prosthesis | Above-the-knee prosthesis | Above-the-knee and hip joint prosthesis |

What Is Prosthetics?

Fill in the circle by the correct answer. Then write the answers to numbers 3, 4, and 5.

1. An individual may consider _____ when choosing an artificial limb.
    Ⓐ material, size, and function
    Ⓑ appearance
    Ⓒ fit
    Ⓓ all of the above

2. The terms "prostheses," "artificial limbs," and "prosthetic limbs" _____.
    Ⓐ are used in different areas of medicine
    Ⓑ relate to leg replacements only
    Ⓒ have completely different meanings
    Ⓓ refer to the same thing

3. Explain the differences between the artificial limbs shown in the text.

    _____

    _____

4. How does the author support the idea that there are different kinds of artificial limbs?

    _____

    _____

5. In your own words, what is the main purpose of artificial limbs?

    _____

    _____

Write About the Topic

Use the Writing Form to write about what you read.

Explain the factors that can influence a person's choice of an artificial limb. Use details from the text.

Prosthetics Innovation

Prosthetics is an area of medicine and surgery that deals with artificial limbs. An artificial limb is a device that a doctor fits onto a person's body to take the place of an arm or leg. Over time, technology has allowed the creation of new and improved artificial limbs.

The Earliest Uses of Prosthetics

There is evidence that ancient Egyptians used prosthetics. In Egypt, a prosthetic toe was found in an archaeological dig. It's estimated to be 3,000 years old and was made of wood and leather. And a historical account states that a warrior from ancient Rome lost his arm in a battle. He then had an iron hand made, which could hold his shield so that he could continue fighting. For hundreds of years, prosthetic devices had uncomplicated designs

World War I veterans with prosthetic arms working in a shop in 1917

with simple materials such as metal, wood, and leather. Knights during the Middle Ages commonly used iron prosthetic limbs. Back then, the purpose of prosthetics was for people to appear as if they weren't missing limbs rather than for the limbs to be functional.

Improvements in Prosthetics

In the 1500s, a French doctor wanted to add joints to artificial limbs. Before then, an artificial limb's ability to perform a function wasn't a big concern. He created the first prosthetic arm with a hinge, which allowed it to bend. He also invented a hinged mechanical hand and a prosthetic leg with a hinge at the knee that could be locked. It also had a harness, which helped it better attach to the body. In 1690, a Dutch doctor created a new kind of prosthetic leg with a cuff that improved how easily the limb attached to the body. These early prosthetic designs influenced prosthetics in the 20th century and today.

Prosthetics Today

Some artificial limbs appear and function so naturally that it's difficult to tell them apart from real body parts. Leather, plastic, and wood are common materials used to make artificial limbs. Computer technology and mechanical pieces are used to design, build, fit, and adjust artificial limbs. These days, prosthetics technology aims to create natural-looking, natural-moving artificial limbs.

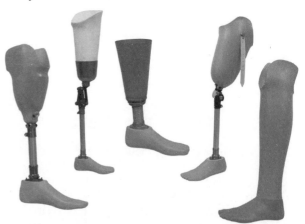

Five different kinds of leg prosthetics

 Nonfiction Reading Practice • EMC 3235 • © Evan-Moor Corp.

Prosthetics Innovation

Fill in the circle by the correct answer. Then write the answers to numbers 3, 4, and 5.

1. What is the main idea of this text?
   Ⓐ Artistic creativity has improved the quality of artificial limbs.
   Ⓑ Technology has improved the quality of artificial limbs over time.
   Ⓒ The earliest uses of prosthetics were better than today's.
   Ⓓ The oldest prosthetic device is 3,000 years old.

2. Why were the earliest artificial limbs more simple?
   Ⓐ Technology wasn't as advanced back then.
   Ⓑ Technology was more advanced back then.
   Ⓒ They didn't have any of the same materials we have now.
   Ⓓ People didn't need artificial limbs back then.

3. What is one possible challenge knights using an iron artificial limb had? Why?

   _____

   _____

4. Which areas of prosthetics technology have seen improvement over the years?

   _____

   _____

5. Are today's prosthetic limbs necessarily better than those of the past? Why or why not?

   _____

   _____

Write About the Topic

Use the Writing Form to write about what you read.

Compare and contrast how prosthetics was in its early days with how it is now. Use details from the text.

Prosthetics: Past and Present

Prosthetics is an area of medicine that deals with artificial limbs, which are sometimes also known as prosthetic limbs. An artificial limb is a device that replaces a person's arm or leg. Artificial limbs have been used for centuries and have changed with technology and with people's ever-changing needs.

Earlier Prosthetics

In 2000, a prosthetic toe was found in an archaeological dig near Thebes, Egypt. It is in a museum in Cairo. It is thought to be about 3,000 years old. And a famous story tells of an ancient Roman general who lost his arm in battle. He then had an iron hand made, which could hold his shield so that he could continue battling. For hundreds of years, prosthetic devices had uncomplicated designs with simple materials such as metal, wood, and leather. Knights during the Middle Ages used iron prosthetic limbs, which were tough but not very flexible. Their purpose wasn't to function as an arm or leg but rather to give the appearance that a limb wasn't missing.

In the 1500s, a doctor invented a prosthetic arm with a hinge, which allowed the arm to bend. He also invented a hinged mechanical hand and a prosthetic leg with a hinge at the knee that could be locked when the user wanted to stand upright. Adding these joint-like features to prosthetic limbs allowed more movement in the limbs. Before then, people didn't expect artificial limbs to perform a function. These early prosthetic designs influenced prosthetics today.

Prosthetics Today

Technology has improved over time, and individuals' needs have changed, so options for artificial limbs have changed, too. We still have artificial limbs that don't allow movement. But there are many other options that didn't exist centuries ago. Some artificial limbs appear and function so naturally that it's difficult to tell them apart from real limbs. Nowadays, people are living longer, healthier lives. People who use artificial limbs do not have to be

An athlete who uses a prosthetic lower limb

limited in their physical activity. This means that artificial limbs need to be more durable and flexible. Luckily, we have computer technology and more sophisticated mechanical pieces to design, build, fit, and adjust artificial limbs. Prosthetics technology aims to create the most naturally functioning prosthetic limbs possible.

          Nonfiction Reading Practice • EMC 3235 • © Evan-Moor Corp.

Prosthetics: Past and Present

Fill in the circle by the correct answer. Then write the answers to numbers 3, 4, and 5.

1. Why did doctors in the 1500s most likely seek to change prosthetics?
   - Ⓐ They wanted to make prosthetics a more popular field of medicine.
   - Ⓑ They thought adding joints could improve the user's movement.
   - Ⓒ Prosthetics technology at that time was extremely advanced.
   - Ⓓ Artificial limbs didn't exist during the Middle Ages.

2. The archaeological discovery in Egypt was significant because it showed that _____.
   - Ⓐ ancient civilizations had knights
   - Ⓑ ancient civilizations had computer technology
   - Ⓒ prosthetics existed in ancient civilizations
   - Ⓓ prosthetics didn't exist thousands of years ago

3. How does the photo support the main idea of the text?

   _____

   _____

4. How have people's expectations of prosthetics changed over time?

   _____

   _____

5. What does the author mean by stating that early prosthetic designs still apply today?

   _____

   _____

Write About the Topic

Use the Writing Form to write about what you read.

Should more advancements in prosthetics be made if current prosthetics already work? Write an argument for why or why not.

Engineers Do Important Work

Level 1 ■

Words to Know list, Reading Selection, and Reading Comprehension questions

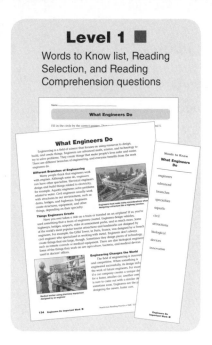

Level 2 ■ ■

Words to Know list, Reading Selection, and Reading Comprehension questions

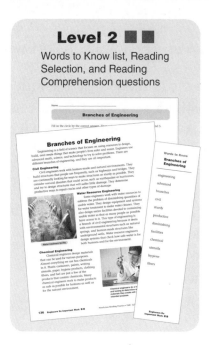

Level 3 ■ ■ ■

Words to Know list, Reading Selection, and Reading Comprehension questions

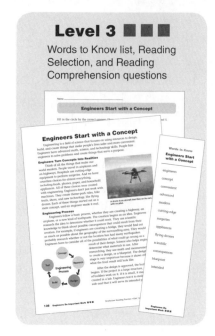

Assemble the Unit

Reproduce and distribute one copy for each student:

- Visual Literacy page: Engineers Do Important Work, page 131
- Level 1, 2, or 3 Reading Selection and Reading Comprehension page and the corresponding Words to Know list
- Graphic Organizer of your choosing, provided on pages 180–186
- Writing Form: Engineers Do Important Work, page 132

Visual Literacy

Introduce the Topic

Read aloud and discuss the Engineers Do Important Work text and photos. Explain that there are many branches of engineering. Point out that some people have the misconception that all engineers work with engines and machines. Explain that engineers design things and try to solve problems.

Read and Respond

Form leveled groups and review the Words to Know lists with each group of students. Instruct each group to read their selection individually, in pairs, or as a group. Have students complete the Reading Comprehension page for their selection.

Writing Form

Write About the Topic

Read aloud the leveled writing prompt for each group. Tell students to use the Graphic Organizer to plan their writing. Direct students to use their Writing Form to respond to their prompt.

Engineers Do Important Work

Engineers use science, math, and technology to solve problems and to create things. Engineers often have specialties. The field of engineering has existed for centuries.

The Step Pyramid in Saqqara, Egypt, is a world-famous landmark. It was built around 2550 BC by a man named Imhotep, who is the world's first engineer identified by name.

The Eiffel Tower was designed by a civil engineer. Civil engineers work structures into natural and human-made environments.

Aeronautical engineers work with aircrafts and the science of flight.

Sustainable or "green" engineers work to create things that help humans while also helping the natural environment.

Name _____

Engineers Do Important Work

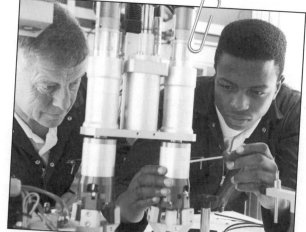

Nonfiction Reading Practice • EMC 3235 • © Evan-Moor Corp.

Words to Know

What Engineers Do

engineers

advanced

branches

specialties

aquatic

civil

attractions

biological

devices

innovative

Engineers Do Important Work ■

Words to Know

Branches of Engineering

engineering

advanced

branches

civil

sturdy

productive

diminishing

facilities

chemical

utensils

hygiene

fibers

Engineers Do Important Work ■ ■

Words to Know

Engineers Start with a Concept

engineers

concept

convenient

advanced

modern

cutting-edge

surgeries

appliances

flying drones

scientific

consequences

blueprint

intended

Engineers Do Important Work ■ ■ ■

What Engineers Do

Engineering is a field of science that focuses on using resources to design, build, and create things. Engineers use advanced math, science, and technology to try to solve problems. They create things that make people's lives safer and easier. There are different branches of engineering, and everyone benefits from the work engineers do.

Different Branches of Engineering

Many people think that engineers work with engines. Although some do, engineers can have other specialties. Electrical engineers design and build things related to electricity, for example. Aquatic engineers solve problems related to water. Civil engineers usually work with structures in our environment, such as dams, bridges, and highways. Engineers create structures, equipment, and other things, depending on their specialty.

Engineers must make many considerations when designing a structure like a highway junction.

Things Engineers Create

Have you ever taken a ride on a train or traveled on an airplane? If so, you've used something that a team of engineers created. Engineers design vehicles, highways, bridges, airports, rides at amusement parks, and so much more. Some of the world's most popular tourist attractions and landmarks are designed by engineers. For example, the Eiffel Tower, in Paris, France, was designed by a French civil engineer who specialized in working with metal. Engineers don't always create things that are large, though. Sometimes they design pieces of technology, such as remote controls or medical equipment. There are also biological engineers. Some of the things they work on are agriculture, bacteria, and medical devices used in doctors' offices.

Medical worker using pharmacy equipment designed by an engineer

Engineering Changes the World

The field of engineering is innovative and competitive. When something is engineered successfully, its design influences the work of future engineers. For example, if a car company creates a unique design for a faster, smaller car, another company is sure to come out with a similar design sometime soon. Engineers are the people designing the newer, faster cars.

  Nonfiction Reading Practice • EMC 3235 • © Evan-Moor Corp.

What Engineers Do

Fill in the circle by the correct answer. Then write the answers to numbers 3, 4, and 5.

1. Air travel would _____ without engineers.
   - Ⓐ continue
   - Ⓑ be safer
   - Ⓒ be impossible
   - Ⓓ be possible

2. A civil engineer probably considers _____ when designing a highway.
   - Ⓐ the amount of sunlight
   - Ⓑ the weight of vehicles
   - Ⓒ how much water is used daily
   - Ⓓ the number of families per U.S. state

3. List two things you've done that were probably possible because of engineering.

   _____

   _____

4. Why do you think engineers are needed in so many different fields and specialties?

   _____

   _____

5. How does the author support the idea that engineering is competitive?

   _____

   _____

Write About the Topic

Use the Writing Form to write about what you read.

> Explain how the world would be different without engineers.
> Use details from the text and your own examples.

Branches of Engineering

Engineering is a field of science that focuses on using resources to design, build, and create things that make people's lives safer and easier. Engineers use advanced math, science, and technology to try to solve problems. There are different branches of engineering, and they are all important.

Civil Engineering

Civil engineers work with human-made and natural environments. They build structures that people use frequently, such as highways and bridges. They are continually looking for ways to make structures as sturdy as possible. They consider natural disasters that could occur, such as earthquakes or hurricanes, and try to design structures that will suffer little damage. They determine productive ways to repair cracks and other types of damage.

Water treatment facility

Water Resource Engineering

Some engineers work with water resources to address the problem of diminishing quantities of usable water. They design equipment and systems for water treatment to make water cleaner. They also design entire facilities devoted to containing usable water so that as many people as possible have access to it. This type of engineering is a branch of civil engineering because it deals with environmental structures such as natural springs and human-made structures like underground wells. Water resource engineers design systems that check how safe water is for both humans and for the environment.

Chemical Engineering

Chemical engineers design materials that can be used for various purposes. Almost everything we use has chemicals in it. Plastic containers, paints, writing utensils, paper, hygiene products, clothing fibers, and fuel are just a few of the products that contain chemicals. Many chemical engineers work to make products as safe as possible for humans as well as for the natural environment.

Chemical engineers do a lot of research and testing to determine whether the materials they create will serve their intended purpose.

Branches of Engineering

Fill in the circle by the correct answer. Then write the answers to numbers 3, 4, and 5.

1. One of a chemical engineer's tasks is to _____.
   - Ⓐ add hazardous chemicals to products
   - Ⓑ build water pipes
   - Ⓒ create large structures
   - Ⓓ make products safe for the environment

2. The main idea of this text is that _____.
   - Ⓐ most engineers work with highways and bridges
   - Ⓑ all branches of engineering are important
   - Ⓒ some branches of engineering are less important
   - Ⓓ all engineers make the world less safe

3. Which type of engineering in the text do you think affects you the most? Explain why.

   _____

   _____

4. Explain why diminishing quantities of usable water is a problem that engineers can help with.

   _____

   _____

5. Explain how the author supports the idea that engineers solve problems.

   _____

   _____

Write About the Topic

Use the Writing Form to write about what you read.

Compare and contrast the branches of engineering discussed in the text. Use details from the text and your own examples.

Engineers Start with a Concept

Engineering is a field of science that focuses on using resources to design, build, and create things that make people's lives safer and more convenient. Engineers have advanced math, science, and technology skills. People hire engineers to solve problems and create things that serve a purpose.

Engineers Turn Concepts Into Realities

Think of all the things that make our world modern. People travel in airplanes and on highways. Hospitals use cutting-edge equipment to perform surgeries. And we have countless choices for almost everything, including foods, phones, paper, and household appliances. All of these choices were created with engineering. Engineers don't just work with machines. They create theme-park rides, bike trails, shoes, and new technology, like flying drones. Each of these things started out as a mere concept, and an engineer made it real.

A drone is an aircraft that flies on its own, with no pilot.

Engineering Process

Engineers follow a basic process, whether they are creating a highway, an airplane, or a new kind of toothpaste. The creation begins as an idea. Engineers research the idea to determine whether it could work. They use scientific knowledge to think about possible consequences that could result from their creation. For example, if engineers are creating a bridge, they would find out as much as possible about the geography of the surrounding area. They would probably research whether or not the location has had many earthquakes. Engineers have to consider all of the possibilities of what could go wrong as a result of their design. Science also helps engineers determine what materials to use. After researching, they use math and measurements to create a design, or a blueprint. The design stage is very important because it shows others what the final result will look like.

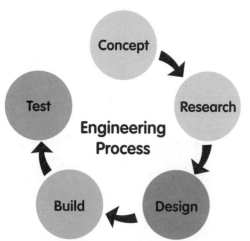

After the design is approved, the building begins. If the project is a large structure, a lot of builders work on it. If it is small, it may be created in a lab. Engineers test it to make sure it's safe and that it will serve its intended purpose.

   Nonfiction Reading Practice • EMC 3235 • © Evan-Moor Corp.

Engineers Start with a Concept

Fill in the circle by the correct answer. Then write the answers to numbers 3, 4, and 5.

1. What does the author mean by stating "an engineer made it real"?
   Ⓐ Engineers are hired by people who need ideas.
   Ⓑ Engineers are the people who usually have good ideas.
   Ⓒ Ideas are real, and objects are not real.
   Ⓓ A concept is just an idea until someone figures out how to build it.

2. Having scientific knowledge helps an engineer to _____.
   Ⓐ determine whether or not to follow the engineering process
   Ⓑ learn more about theme parks
   Ⓒ create a design that could work in its environment
   Ⓓ learn more about rules at hospitals

3. List some things that you use that were probably designed by an engineer.

   _____

   _____

4. Why is it important for engineers to use a process?

   _____

   _____

5. If the final product failed the testing stage, what do you think an engineer would do?

   _____

   _____

Write About the Topic

Use the Writing Form to write about what you read.

Think of something created by an engineer. Explain how an engineer used the process to create it and what considerations the engineer probably made. Use text details.

Inventions Impact Our Lives

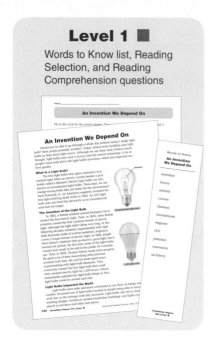
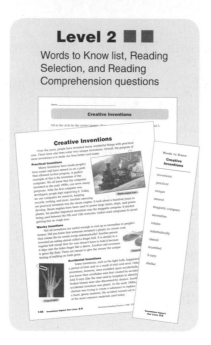
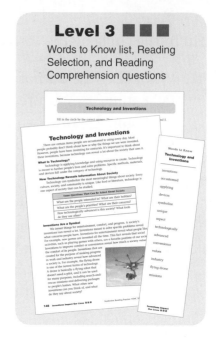
Assemble the Unit

Reproduce and distribute one copy for each student:

- Visual Literacy page: Inventions Impact Our Lives, page 141
- Level 1, 2, or 3 Reading Selection and Reading Comprehension page and the corresponding Words to Know list
- Graphic Organizer of your choosing, provided on pages 180–186
- Writing Form: Inventions Impact Our Lives, page 142

Introduce the Topic

Read aloud and discuss the Inventions Impact Our Lives photos and paragraphs. Ask students to mention some inventions or inventors they know of. Explain that all inventions start out as mere ideas. Point out that many inventions are improved upon with technology after they are first created.

Read and Respond

Form leveled groups and review the Words to Know lists with each group of students. Instruct each group to read their selection individually, in pairs, or as a group. Have students complete the Reading Comprehension page for their selection.

Write About the Topic

Read aloud the leveled writing prompt for each group. Tell students to use the Graphic Organizer to plan their writing. Direct students to use their Writing Form to respond to their prompt.

Visual Literacy

Writing Form

Inventions Impact Our Lives

Inventions make our lives better. Most inventions are not created by a single person. Instead, an invention is usually the result of many small improvements made to an original product over time by more than one person.

Some inventions end up being so useful that they become household necessities or change the way society functions. The light bulb is a great example of this kind of significant invention.

Other inventions are unique and fun, but not as widely used.

Thomas Edison in his laboratory, circa 1901

A fork and spoon combined to make a "spork"

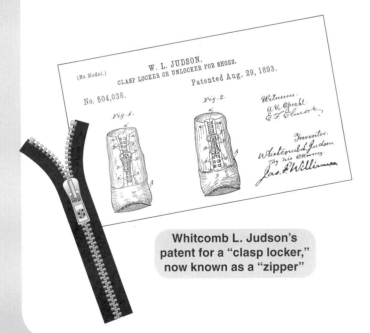

Whitcomb L. Judson's patent for a "clasp locker," now known as a "zipper"

A hands-free umbrella known as an "umbrella hat"

Name _____

Inventions Impact Our Lives

_____
_____
_____
_____
_____

_____
_____
_____
_____
_____
_____
_____
_____
_____
_____
_____
_____
_____

Words to Know	Words to Know	Words to Know
An Invention We Depend On	**Creative Inventions**	**Technology and Inventions**
invention	inventions	inventions
luxury	practical	accustomed
emitted	unique	applying
current	steered	devices
filament	magnetic compass	symbolize
incandescent	necessities	unique
engineer	rotates	aspect
LED	automatically	technologically
patented	utensil	advanced
convenient	stumbled	convenience
architects	X-rays	values
	shellac	industry
		flying drone
		missions
Inventions Impact Our Lives ■	**Inventions Impact Our Lives** ■ ■	**Inventions Impact Our Lives** ■ ■ ■

An Invention We Depend On

Would you be able to go through a whole day without using a single light bulb? Most people probably wouldn't. Today, almost every building uses light bulbs as their main light source. Although we use them daily without much thought, light bulbs were once a luxury and the newest technology. A lot of people's hard work led to the light bulb's invention, which has impacted our lives greatly.

What Is a Light Bulb?

The first light bulbs were glass containers that emitted light when an electric current heated a part inside called a filament. Electric light bulbs are also known as incandescent light bulbs. These days, we use energy-saving bulbs that are better for the environment. Nick Holonyak, Jr., an American engineer, invented the first light-emitting diode (LED) in 1962. An LED light bulb uses one-third the electricity as an incandescent and lasts far longer.

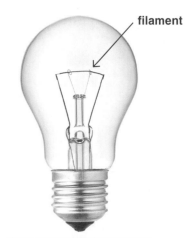

filament

Incandescent light bulb

The Invention of the Light Bulb

In 1802, a British scientist named Humphry Davy created the first electric light. Then, in 1835, other British scientists created the first constant stream of electric light, although the light didn't shine very long. In the following decades, scientists experimented with light bulb filaments made of various materials, hoping to create a longer stream of electric light. In 1860, Joseph Swan found a material that produced a good light, but it burned out quickly. By this time, none of the light bulbs created were ready to be sold to the public for everyday use. Then, in 1878, Thomas Edison made more progress. He spent a lot of time researching what previous scientists had done. He and his team spent years experimenting with light bulb filaments. They eventually created the first light bulb that could emit constant electric light for 1,200 hours. Edison immediately patented his light bulb design so that light bulbs could be created and sold.

LED light bulb

Light Bulbs Impacted the World

Light bulbs were safer and more convenient to use than oil lamps and candles. Increased use of light bulbs resulted in people being able to have a longer work day, so the average work day increased. Light bulbs also led to changes in building designs. Architects created windowless buildings, and lights could be placed in elevators and other new places.

An Invention We Depend On

Fill in the circle by the correct answer. Then write the answers to numbers 3, 4, and 5.

1. Joseph Swan was probably _____.
   Ⓐ a candle maker
   Ⓑ a customer
   Ⓒ an architect
   Ⓓ a scientist

2. Why does the author state that light bulbs were a "luxury"?
   Ⓐ They weren't common.
   Ⓑ They were viewed similarly to how they're viewed today.
   Ⓒ They didn't change the things that people were able to do.
   Ⓓ Everyone had them in their homes during the 1800s.

3. Write one of the main ideas of the text.

   _____

   _____

4. Why was it significant that lights could be placed in new places such as elevators?

   _____

   _____

5. Why do you think scientists spent so much time creating a constant stream of light?

   _____

   _____

Write About the Topic

Use the Writing Form to write about what you read.

> Who should receive credit for the invention of the light bulbs we use today? Write an argument using details from the text.

Creative Inventions

Over the years, people have invented many wonderful things with practical uses. There have also been some very unique inventions. Overall, the purpose of most inventions is to make our lives better and easier.

Practical Inventions

Many inventions have made people's lives easier and have steered us on a path that allowed further progress. A perfect example of this is the invention of the computer. We all know that the computer, invented in the early 1900s, can serve many purposes. After the first computer was developed, people kept improving it. Today, we use computers for research, keeping records, writing, and more. Another amazing

Steam engine train

yet practical invention was the steam engine. It took about a hundred years to develop. Steam engines have been used to power large trains, ships, and power plants. Yet another important invention was the magnetic compass. It started being used between the 9th and 11th centuries. Sailors used compasses to avoid getting lost on rough seas.

Wacky Inventions

Not all inventions are useful enough to end up as necessities in people's homes. Did you know that someone invented a plastic ice cream cone that rotates the ice cream scoop automatically? Another person invented an eating utensil called a finger fork. It is similar to a regular fork except that the user doesn't have to hold it because it slips onto the index finger like a sleeve. Another odd invention is grass flip-flops. These are meant to give the wearer the unique feeling of walking on fresh grass.

Grass flip-flops

Accidental Inventions

Some inventions, such as the light bulb, happened over a period of time and as a result of trial and error. Other inventions, however, were stumbled upon accidentally. Did you know that cornflakes were first created by accident? And X-rays (like the ones used in hospitals to identify broken bones) were also discovered by chance. Another accidental invention was plastic. In the early 1900s, a chemist was trying to create a substance to replace shellac, a hard, glossy material. His accident turned out to be one of the most common materials used today.

X-ray of hand

Nonfiction Reading Practice • EMC 3235 • © Evan-Moor Corp.

Creative Inventions

Fill in the circle by the correct answer. Then write the answers to numbers 3, 4, and 5.

1. The main idea of the text is that _____.
   - Ⓐ people invent things for no specific reason
   - Ⓑ inventions make our lives easier and better
   - Ⓒ inventions are usually silly and fun
   - Ⓓ all inventions have practical uses

2. People invent things _____.
   - Ⓐ for many different purposes
   - Ⓑ mainly for attention
   - Ⓒ mostly for comfort
   - Ⓓ for work

3. Is an invention more, less, or equally valuable if created by accident? Explain why.

   _____

   _____

4. What does the author mean by stating that some inventions allowed further progress?

   _____

   _____

5. Which of the "wacky" inventions did you find most surprising, and why?

   _____

   _____

Write About the Topic

Use the Writing Form to write about what you read.

Describe what the world would be like if people didn't invent new things. Use your own examples and details from the text.

Technology and Inventions

There are certain items people are accustomed to using every day. Most people probably don't think about how or why the things we use were invented. However, people have been inventing for centuries. It's important to think about these inventions, because technology can reveal a lot about the society that uses it.

What Is Technology?

Technology is applying knowledge and using resources to create. Technology is meant to further people's lives and solve problems. Specific methods, materials, and devices fall under the category of technology.

How Technology Reveals Information About Society

Technology can symbolize the most meaningful things about society. Every culture, society, and community is unique. Like food or literature, technology is one aspect of society that can be studied.

Some Questions That Can Be Asked About Society
What are the people interested in? What are their hobbies?
What are the people's priorities? What are their concerns?
How technologically advanced is this society? What tools do they use often?

Inventions Are a Symbol

We invent things for entertainment, comfort, and progress. A society's inventions can reveal a lot. Inventions meant to solve specific problems reveal what concerns people have. Inventions for entertainment reveal what people like. For example, new games are invented all the time. This fact reveals that social activities, such as playing games with others, are a favorite pastime of our society. Inventions to improve comfort or convenience reveal how much a society values the comfort of its people. Inventions that are created for the purpose of making progress in work and industry reveal how advanced a society is. For example, the flying drone is one of the newest forms of technology. A drone is basically a flying robot that doesn't need a pilot, and it can be used for many purposes, including search-and-rescue missions and delivering packages to people's homes. What other new inventions can you think of, and what do they say about society?

Technology and Inventions

Fill in the circle by the correct answer. Then write the answers to numbers 3, 4, and 5.

1. A search-and-rescue drone would likely be used to _____.
   - Ⓐ protect people from natural disasters
   - Ⓑ help with food preparation
   - Ⓒ go to locations that are too dangerous for people
   - Ⓓ make people feel comfortable in their homes

2. Why does the author include the questions in the table?
   - Ⓐ These are the only important questions about society.
   - Ⓑ The answers to all the questions can be found in the text.
   - Ⓒ The author wants readers to memorize the answers to the questions.
   - Ⓓ The questions encourage readers to think about different aspects of society.

3. How does the author support the idea that technology reveals information about society?

   _____

   _____

4. Write one of the main ideas from the text.

   _____

   _____

5. People have invented things for centuries. What does this say about us?

   _____

   _____

Write About the Topic

Use the Writing Form to write about what you read.

What can you infer about a community from looking at its technology? Use a specific community as an example.

Augusta Savage

Level 1 ■

Words to Know list, Reading Selection, and Reading Comprehension questions

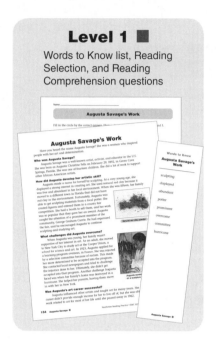

Level 2 ■ ■

Words to Know list, Reading Selection, and Reading Comprehension questions

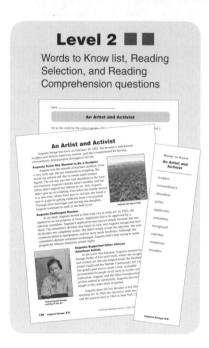

Level 3 ■ ■ ■

Words to Know list, Reading Selection, and Reading Comprehension questions

Assemble the Unit

Reproduce and distribute one copy for each student:

- Visual Literacy page: Augusta Savage, page 151
- Level 1, 2, or 3 Reading Selection and Reading Comprehension page and the corresponding Words to Know list
- Graphic Organizer of your choosing, provided on pages 180–186
- Writing Form: Augusta Savage, page 152

Introduce the Topic

Read aloud and discuss the Augusta Savage text and photos. Explain that Augusta was an important person in African American history because she helped make art more accessible to African Americans, and she portrayed African Americans in her art.

Read and Respond

Form leveled groups and review the Words to Know lists with each group of students. Instruct each group to read their selection individually, in pairs, or as a group. Have students complete the Reading Comprehension page for their selection.

Write About the Topic

Read aloud the leveled writing prompt for each group. Tell students to use the Graphic Organizer to plan their writing. Direct students to use their Writing Form to respond to their prompt.

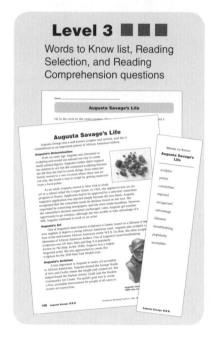

Visual Literacy

Writing Form

150

Augusta Savage

Augusta Savage was a well-known sculptor and activist. She is remembered for her extraordinary determination, art, and activism. Augusta was an important artist and person in African American history.

Augusta began sculpting with natural red clay, which was abundant in the local environment where she grew up.

Natural red clay powder

Augusta standing beside
one of her sculptures

Augusta Savage's best-known work of
the 1920s was this sculpture, *Gamin*.

Augusta Savage

_____

_____

_____

_____

_____

_____

_____

_____

_____

_____

_____

_____

_____

_____

_____

_____

_____

_____

_____

_____

Augusta Savage's Work

sculpting

displayed

abundant

potter

prominent

overcome

committee

hurricane

An Artist and Activist

sculptor

extraordinary

abundant

potter

applicants

committee

recognized

rejection

numerous

founders

Augusta Savage's Life

sculptor

potter

committee

rejected

recognized

advantage

likeness

breathtaking

popularly

accessible

Augusta Savage ■

Augusta Savage ■ ■

Augusta Savage ■ ■ ■

Augusta Savage's Work

Have you heard the name Augusta Savage? She was a woman who inspired people with her art and determination.

Who was Augusta Savage?

Augusta Savage was a well-known artist, activist, and educator in the U.S. She was born as Augusta Christine Fells on February 29, 1892, in Green Cove Springs, Florida. She was one of fourteen children. She did a lot of work to support other African American artists.

How did Augusta develop her artistic skill?

Augusta made a name for herself by sculpting. At a very young age, she displayed a strong interest in creating art. She used natural red clay because it was free and abundant in her local environment. When she was fifteen, her family moved to a different town in Florida that did not have red clay in the environment. Fortunately, Augusta was able to get sculpting materials from a local potter. She created figures and entered them in a county fair competition. She had a booth to sell them, and her work was so popular that they gave her an award. Augusta caught the attention of a prominent member of the community, George Graham Currie. He had organized the fair, and he encouraged Augusta to continue sculpting and studying art.

Natural red clay powder

What challenges did Augusta overcome?

When Augusta was young, her family wasn't supportive of her interest in art. As an adult, she moved to New York City to study art at the Cooper Union, a school for science and art. In 1923, Augusta applied for a learning program overseas, in France. She was rejected by a selection committee because of racism. This made her more determined to be accepted into the program. She contacted local newspapers and tried to challenge the injustice done to her. Ultimately, she didn't get accepted into that program. Another challenge Augusta faced was when her family's home was destroyed in a hurricane. She helped her parents, having them move in with her in New York.

Augusta working intently on a sculpture

Was Augusta's art career successful?

Augusta influenced other artists and taught art for many years. Her own art career didn't provide enough income for her to live off of, but she was able to do work related to art for most of her life until she passed away in 1962.

   Nonfiction Reading Practice • EMC 3235 • © Evan-Moor Corp.

Augusta Savage's Work

Fill in the circle by the correct answer. Then write the answers to numbers 3, 4, and 5.

1. Augusta showed determination by _____.
   - Ⓐ sculpting with her thirteen siblings
   - Ⓑ using red clay to create sculptures
   - Ⓒ finding a way to sculpt after not being able to get red clay
   - Ⓓ spending money on expensive sculpting materials

2. In the photo, Augusta appears as though she is probably _____.
   - Ⓐ content
   - Ⓑ confused
   - Ⓒ stressed out
   - Ⓓ bored

3. Do you think the county fair was an important event in Augusta's life? Why or why not?

   _____

   _____

4. Did Augusta respond appropriately to the selection committee's decision? Why or why not?

   _____

   _____

5. Why do you think Augusta supported other African American artists?

   _____

   _____

Write About the Topic

Use the Writing Form to write about what you read.

Explain how Augusta showed determination in pursuing her interests despite obstacles. Use details from the text.

An Artist and Activist

Augusta Savage was born on February 29, 1892. She became a well-known sculptor and African American activist, and she is remembered for having extraordinary determination throughout her life.

Augusta Knew She Wanted to Be a Sculptor

Augusta was the seventh of fourteen children. From a very early age, she was interested in sculpting. She would use natural red clay to create small animal figures. The red clay was free and abundant in the local environment. Augusta's family wasn't wealthy, and her father didn't support her interest in art. Still, Augusta didn't give up on sculpting. Even when her family moved to a new town, where there was no red clay, she found a way to sculpt by getting materials from a local potter. Through three marriages and having one daughter, Augusta continued to work in the field of art.

Natural red clay in field

Augusta Challenged Racism

As an adult, Augusta moved to New York City to study art. In 1923, she applied for an art program in France. Applicants had to be approved by a selection committee. Augusta's application was rejected simply because she was black. The committee's decision was based on race, and Augusta recognized that its decision was completely unfair. She didn't simply accept the rejection. She sent numerous letters to newspapers, and her story made headlines. Although the committee's decision remained unchanged, Augusta didn't stop trying to make progress for African American artists' rights.

Young Augusta Savage working on her art

Augusta Supported Other African American Artists

In the years that followed, Augusta started the Savage Studio of Arts and Crafts, where she taught and created art. She also helped found the Harlem Artists' Guild and the Harlem Community Art Center. The guild's goal was to create a free, accessible environment for people of all races to receive art instruction. Augusta and the other founders believed art was central to community. Augusta directed and taught at the center when it opened.

Augusta spent the last decades of her life teaching art. In 1960, she moved in with her daughter, and she passed away in 1962 in New York City.

Nonfiction Reading Practice • EMC 3235 • © Evan-Moor Corp.

An Artist and Activist

Fill in the circle by the correct answer. Then write the answers to numbers 3, 4, and 5.

1. It was difficult for Augusta to develop her sculpting skills _____.
   Ⓐ with red clay
   Ⓑ at the Harlem Community Art Center
   Ⓒ at the Savage Studio of Arts and Crafts
   Ⓓ with little support from her father

2. Augusta was the director of the art center most likely because _____.
   Ⓐ she had the least amount of experience with art
   Ⓑ she was passionate about supporting other African American artists
   Ⓒ nobody else believed in the cause of supporting other artists
   Ⓓ free art instruction wouldn't provide a large income

3. Describe how Augusta responded to struggles in her life.

   _____

   _____

4. How does the author support the idea that Augusta was an activist?

   _____

   _____

5. What do you admire or dislike about Augusta Savage? Explain why.

   _____

   _____

Write About the Topic

Use the Writing Form to write about what you read.

Describe three personality traits that you think Augusta had, and support these statements using text details.

Augusta Savage's Life

Augusta Savage was a well-known sculptor and activist, and she is remembered as an important person in African American history.

Augusta's Determination

From an early age, Augusta was interested in sculpting and would use natural red clay to create small animal figures. Augusta's father didn't support her interest in art, but she continued sculpting because she felt that she had to create things. Even when her family moved to a new location where there was no red clay, she found a way to sculpt by getting materials from a local potter.

As an adult, Augusta moved to New York to study art at a school called the Cooper Union. In 1923, she applied to join an art program in France. Applicants had to be approved by a selection committee. Augusta's application was rejected simply because she was black. Augusta recognized that the committee made its decision based on her race. She responded by contacting newspapers, and her story made headlines. However, the committee's decision remained unchanged. Later, Augusta got another opportunity to go overseas, although she was unable to take advantage of it. Still, Augusta continued to work as an artist.

Augusta's Art

One of Augusta's most famous sculptures is *Gamin*, based on a likeness of her own nephew. It depicts a young African American man. Augusta also sculpted a bust of the well-known African American writer W.E.B. Du Bois. She often sculpted likenesses of African American leaders. One of Augusta's most breathtaking sculptures was *Lift Every Voice and Sing*. It is popularly known as *The Harp*. In the 1930s, Augusta was a highly respected artist. She was approached to create this sculpture for the 1939 New York World's Fair.

Augusta's Activism

It was important to Augusta to make art accessible to African Americans. Augusta started the Savage Studio of Arts and Crafts, where she taught and created art. She helped found the Harlem Artists' Guild and the Harlem Community Art Center. The guild's goal was to create a free, accessible environment for people of all races to receive art instruction.

Gamin

Augusta's best-known work in the 1920s was a bust of her nephew.

Nonfiction Reading Practice • EMC 3235 • © Evan-Moor Corp.

Augusta Savage's Life

Fill in the circle by the correct answer. Then write the answers to numbers 3, 4, and 5.

1. Augusta was probably hopeful that contacting newspapers would _____.
   - Ⓐ encourage the selection committee to change its decision
   - Ⓑ make newspaper readers more interested in art
   - Ⓒ make the committee cancel the art program in France
   - Ⓓ encourage the selection committee to reject other applicants, too

2. Augusta's art and activism most likely _____.
   - Ⓐ caused her nephew to be embarrassed
   - Ⓑ allowed fewer African Americans to become artists
   - Ⓒ encouraged more writers to ask for busts of themselves
   - Ⓓ helped change perceptions of African Americans for the better

3. Explain why it was probably important for Augusta to make art accessible to all races.

   _____

   _____

4. Write one question you would ask Augusta if you could interview her today.

   _____

   _____

5. Describe the sculpture *Gamin*. What feeling do you get from it?

   _____

   _____

Write About the Topic

Use the Writing Form to write about what you read.

Explain how Augusta affected future generations with her work. Use details and examples to support your answer.

Art or Garbage?

Level 1 ■
Words to Know list, Reading Selection, and Reading Comprehension questions

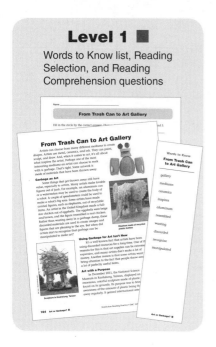

Level 2 ■ ■
Words to Know list, Reading Selection, and Reading Comprehension questions

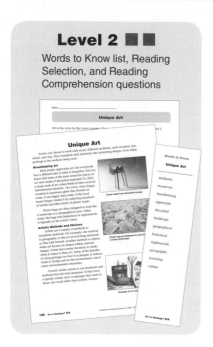

Level 3 ■ ■ ■
Words to Know list, Reading Selection, and Reading Comprehension questions

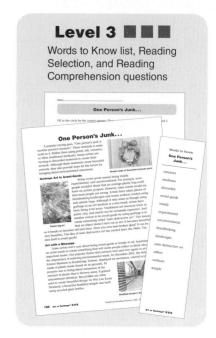

Assemble the Unit

Reproduce and distribute one copy for each student:

- Visual Literacy page: Art or Garbage?, page 161
- Level 1, 2, or 3 Reading Selection and Reading Comprehension page and the corresponding Words to Know list
- Graphic Organizer of your choosing, provided on pages 180–186
- Writing Form: Art or Garbage?, page 162

Introduce the Topic

Read aloud and discuss the Art or Garbage? paragraph and photos. Explain that many discarded items are used by artists to create beautiful works of art. Point out that artists have done this for many years, and there are multiple reasons why an artist might choose to do this.

Read and Respond

Form leveled groups and review the Words to Know lists with each group of students. Instruct each group to read their selection individually, in pairs, or as a group. Have students complete the Reading Comprehension page for their selection.

Write About the Topic

Read aloud the leveled writing prompt for each group. Tell students to use the Graphic Organizer to plan their writing. Direct students to use their Writing Form to respond to their prompt.

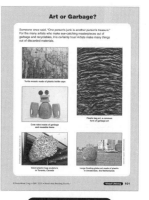

Visual Literacy

Writing Form

Art or Garbage?

Someone once said, "One person's junk is another person's treasure." For the many artists who make eye-catching masterpieces out of garbage and recyclables, it is certainly true! Artists make many things out of discarded materials.

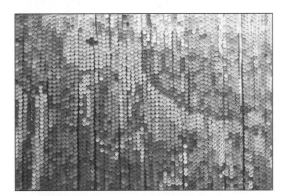

Turtle mosaic made of plastic bottle caps

Plastic bag art, a common form of garbage art

Cute robot made of garbage and reusable items

Giant plastic bag sculpture in Toronto, Canada

Large floating globe art made of plastic in Amsterdam, the Netherlands

Name _____

Art or Garbage?

_____

_____

_____

_____

_____

_____

_____

_____

_____

_____

_____

_____

          _____

          _____

          _____

          _____

          _____

          _____

          _____

Nonfiction Reading Practice • EMC 3235 • © Evan-Moor Corp.

Words to Know

From Trash Can to Art Gallery

gallery

mediums

ceramics

inspires

aluminum

resembled

wasting

discarded

recognize

manipulated

Art or Garbage? ■

Words to Know

Unique Art

mediums

transform

breathtaking

appreciate

discarded

landscape

geographical

fantastical

nightmarish

pyrography

scorching

cubism

Art or Garbage? ■■

Words to Know

One Person's Junk...

ceramics

mediums

discarded

avant-garde

trendy

experimental

unconventional

breathtaking

landscapes

auto-destructive art

reflect

surfaces

temple

Art or Garbage? ■■■

From Trash Can to Art Gallery

Artists can choose from many different mediums to create shapes. Artists use metal, ceramics, and ink. They can paint, sculpt, and draw. And, when it comes to art, it's all about what inspires the artist. Perhaps one of the most interesting mediums an artist can choose to work with is garbage. That's right. Some artwork is made of materials that have been thrown away.

Garbage as Art

Some things that get thrown away still have value, especially to artists. Many artists make lovable figures out of junk. For example, an aluminum can or a watermelon may be used to create the body of a robot. A couple of speedometers could be used to make a robot's big eyes. Some artists have made animal figures, such as elephants, out of recyclable items. An artist in the United Kingdom made a full-sized chicken out of eggshells. The eggshells were beige and brown, and the figure resembled a real chicken. Rather than wasting away in a garbage dump, these discarded materials are used to create images and figures that are pleasing to the eye. But when did artists start to recognize that garbage can be manipulated to make art?

Elephant made of recycled plastic bottles

Sculpture in Kaohsiung, Taiwan

Using Garbage for Art Isn't New

It's a well-known fact that artists have been using discarded resources for a long time. One of the reasons for this is that art supplies can be extremely expensive, and many artists don't make a lot of money. Another reason is that some artists want to bring attention to the fact that people throw away a lot of perfectly useful items.

Art with a Purpose

In December 2011, the National Science Museum in Kaohsiung, Taiwan, displayed an enormous, colorful sculpture made of plastic waste found on its grounds. Its purpose was to bring about awareness of the amount of plastic being thrown away regularly. It gained international attention.

From Trash Can to Art Gallery

Fill in the circle by the correct answer. Then write the answers to numbers 3, 4, and 5.

1. One thing the artwork in all the photos has in common is probably that _____.
   - Ⓐ none of the artwork is pleasing to the eye
   - Ⓑ all of the artwork is made of plastic only
   - Ⓒ the artists felt like they had no choice of mediums
   - Ⓓ the artists were inspired by the mediums they used

2. The purpose of this text is to _____.
   - Ⓐ inform about garbage being used for art
   - Ⓑ persuade that garbage makes better art
   - Ⓒ entertain with a story about garbage
   - Ⓓ teach the process of making art out of garbage

3. Do any photos in the text show art you'd want in your home? Explain why or why not.

   _____

   _____

4. Which would an artist prefer to use as a medium: garbage, clay, or paint? Explain why.

   _____

   _____

5. Explain how the sculpture in Taiwan would encourage awareness about plastic waste.

   _____

   _____

Write About the Topic

Use the Writing Form to write about what you read.

> Would the artwork in the photos be better if it wasn't made of discarded items? Support your opinion with text details.

Unique Art

Artists can choose to work with many different mediums, such as paint, ink, metal, and clay. They transform dull materials into interesting shapes, even when garbage is the medium being used.

Breathtaking Art

Most people appreciate art, but everybody has a different idea of what is beautiful. Did you know that some of the most attractive pieces of art were made of discarded materials? In 2012, a large work of art called *World of Litter* received international attention. The artist, Peter Singer, created an enormous globe that floated on water. It was bigger than some of the local boats! Singer created it by collecting hundreds of bottles and other forms of plastic waste.

Camel made from discarded scraps

Plastic bags are often designed to look like a landscape or a geographical area. Other times, the bags look fantastical or nightmarish. It depends on the artist's vision.

Artistic Methods and Choices

Artists use a variety of methods to transform materials. For example, one method is pyrography, or the art of scorching materials so they look burned. Another method is cubism, when art focuses on shapes within natural images. Artists have many decisions to make when it comes to their art. Some of the benefits of using garbage are that it is cheaper, it reduces waste in dumps and in the environment, and it raises environmental awareness.

Plastic bag art designed to look like a snowy landscape

Ron Ellis / Shutterstock.com

Overall, artists choose to use mediums and methods that suit their purposes. If they have a specific artistic style or message they want to share, this could affect their artistic choices.

Example of art with cubism

Unique Art

Fill in the circle by the correct answer. Then write the answers to numbers 3, 4, and 5.

1. The author probably decided on the title "Unique Art" because _____.
   Ⓐ using garbage reduces waste
   Ⓑ garbage is the only unique medium
   Ⓒ art created from garbage is usually one-of-a-kind
   Ⓓ plastic bag art has to be unique

2. One reason that Peter Singer created *World of Litter* could have been to _____.
   Ⓐ create art that also serves as water transportation
   Ⓑ spend time cleaning plastic bottles
   Ⓒ teach other people how to become artists
   Ⓓ raise awareness about environmental waste

3. Write two questions the text raised for you but didn't answer.

   _____

   _____

4. Describe one image shown in the text that you liked or found interesting.

   _____

   _____

5. Explain in your own words the difference between artistic methods and art mediums.

   _____

   _____

Write About the Topic

Use the Writing Form to write about what you read.

Write a short essay persuading artists why they should use garbage in their art. Use your own examples and text details.

One Person's Junk...

A popular saying goes, "One person's junk is another person's treasure." There certainly is some truth in it. Rather than using paint, ink, ceramics, or other traditional mediums, many artists are turning to discarded materials to create their artwork. Although these materials create beautiful artwork, they also provide hope for the future by bringing about environmental awareness.

Wreath made of discarded computer parts

Garbage Art Is Avant-Garde

Plastic bag art

Being avant-garde means being trendy, experimental, and unconventional. For example, most people wouldn't think that an average plastic bag could have an artistic purpose. However, some artists would say that most people are wrong. Artists have taken photos of breathtaking landscapes and ocean surfaces created using only plastic bags. Although it may seem as though using garbage as an art medium is a new trend, artists have been doing it for years. Traditional art resources (such as paint, clay, and metal) can be extremely expensive. And another reason to be avant-garde by using garbage is to create something called "auto-destructive art." This means that an object doesn't start out as art. It becomes beautiful as it breaks or becomes old and worn. Have you ever seen broken glass? It can be very beautiful. The idea of auto-destructive art has existed since the 1960s. The idea itself is avant-garde!

Art with a Message

Some artists don't care about being avant-garde or trendy at all. Sometimes, an artist wants to create something that will make people reflect or think about important issues. One popular theme that surfaces over and over again in art is the importance of reducing environmental waste. In December 2011, the National Science Museum in Kaohsiung, Taiwan, displayed an enormous, colorful sculpture made of plastic waste found on its grounds. Its purpose was to bring about awareness of the amount of plastic that is thrown away. It gained international attention. Recyclables are often used to create beautiful things. In Wat Lan Kuad, Thailand, a beautiful Buddhist temple was built using recycled glass bottles.

Buddhist temple in Wat Lan Kuad, Thailand

Nonfiction Reading Practice • EMC 3235 • © Evan-Moor Corp.

One Person's Junk...

Fill in the circle by the correct answer. Then write the answers to numbers 3, 4, and 5.

1. The main idea of this text is that _____.
   Ⓐ art that is avant-garde can't have a message
   Ⓑ discarded items can be used to make art
   Ⓒ only plastic bag art can be avant-garde
   Ⓓ auto-destructive art always has a message

2. An example of auto-destructive art could be a _____.
   Ⓐ rusty tricycle in a yard with plants growing around it
   Ⓑ finger painting hanging on a clean wall
   Ⓒ red jar filled with beans on a fresh white doily
   Ⓓ framed drawing of a tree

3. Do you agree with the author about the popular saying quoted in the text? Why or why not?

   _____

   _____

4. How did the author support the idea that garbage art is avant-garde?

   _____

   _____

5. What does artwork with traditional mediums have in common with garbage artwork?

   _____

   _____

Write About the Topic

Use the Writing Form to write about what you read.

Is all garbage art avant-garde or sharing an important message? Write an argument for why or why not.

Ice Hotels

Level 1 ■

Words to Know list, Reading Selection, and Reading Comprehension questions

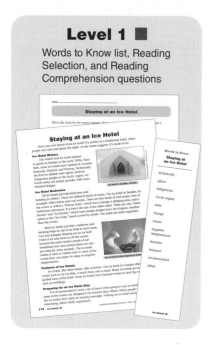

Level 2 ■ ■

Words to Know list, Reading Selection, and Reading Comprehension questions

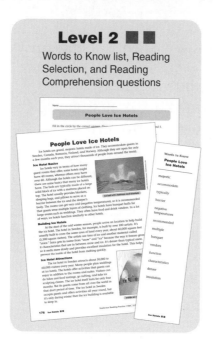

Level 3 ■ ■ ■

Words to Know list, Reading Selection, and Reading Comprehension questions

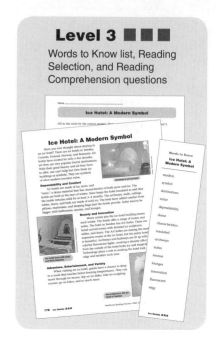

Assemble the Unit

Reproduce and distribute one copy for each student:

- Visual Literacy page: Ice Hotels, page 171
- Level 1, 2, or 3 Reading Selection and Reading Comprehension page and the corresponding Words to Know list
- Graphic Organizer of your choosing, provided on pages 180–186
- Writing Form: Ice Hotels, page 172

Introduce the Topic

Read aloud and discuss the Ice Hotels text and photos. Explain that visiting an ice hotel would be a unique traveling experience. Point out that ice hotels have many similarities to traditional hotels. Explain that ice hotels are considered works of art, but they only last during winter months.

Read and Respond

Form leveled groups and review the Words to Know lists with each group of students. Instruct each group to read their selection individually, in pairs, or as a group. Have students complete the Reading Comprehension page for their selection.

Write About the Topic

Read aloud the leveled writing prompt for each group. Tell students to use the Graphic Organizer to plan their writing. Direct students to use their Writing Form to respond to their prompt.

Visual Literacy

Writing Form

Nonfiction Reading Practice • EMC 3235 • © Evan-Moor Corp.

Ice Hotels

Ice hotels are grand, majestic hotels made of ice. The world's first ice hotel opened to guests in Sweden in the early 1990s. Since then, more ice hotels opened in Canada, Romania, Finland, and Norway.

karenfoleyphotography / Shutterstock.com

Jorg Hackemann / Shutterstock.com

Ice hotels are beautiful. Artists hand carve the rooms, corridors, and sculptures inside the hotel. Lighting experts use fluorescent lights to display bright colors on the hotel's icy surfaces.

Ice hotel beds are made of solid blocks of ice. Mattresses, blankets, sleeping bags, and pillows are placed on top of the beds to make them warmer.

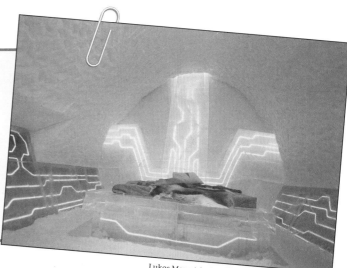

Lukas Maverick Greyson / Shutterstock.com

Name _____

Ice Hotels

_____

_____

_____

_____

_____

_____

_____

_____

_____

_____

_____

_____

_____

_____

_____

_____

_____

_____

Jorg Hackemann / Shutterstock.com

Nonfiction Reading Practice • EMC 3235 • © Evan-Moor Corp.

Words to Know	Words to Know	Words to Know
Staying at an Ice Hotel	**People Love Ice Hotels**	**Ice Hotel: A Modern Symbol**

technically	majestic	modern
igloos	accommodate	symbol
indigenous	typically	destinations
Arctic region	barrier	value
suite	negative temperatures	dependability
lounge	recommended	dense
sauna	multiple	characteristics
negative temperatures	banquet	insulated
features	vendors	archways
banquet	function	suites
recommended	characteristics	saunas
albeit	denser	lounges
	insulation	innovation
		fluorescent
		edgy

Ice Hotels ■	**Ice Hotels** ■ ■	**Ice Hotels** ■ ■ ■

Staying at an Ice Hotel

Have you ever heard of an ice hotel? It's similar to a traditional hotel, where people can visit and spend the night. As the name suggests, it's made of ice.

Ice Hotel History

Ice hotel in Quebec, Canada

The world's first ice hotel opened to guests in Sweden in the early 1990s. Since then, more ice hotels have opened in Canada, Romania, Finland, and Norway. Technically, the first ice shelters were igloos, built by indigenous people in the Arctic region. Ice hotels today are simply grander, with more detailed designs.

Ice Hotel Bedrooms

All ice hotels provide bedrooms and bedding to visitors. There are different kinds of rooms. The ice hotel in Sweden, for example, offers warm and cool rooms. There are five kinds of cool rooms. One of the rooms is called a "Deluxe Suite," which has a lounge, a sleeping area, and a bathroom and sauna. It is twice the size of the other suites. There are also "Snow Rooms" and "Ice Rooms," which have simple designs but a lot of space. Another option is the "Art Suite," hand-carved by artists. The suites are more expensive than the rooms.

An Art Suite at the original ice hotel in Sweden

Most ice hotels provide a mattress and sleeping bags on top of ice beds in each room. Can you imagine sleeping on an ice bed? There is ice and snow in all the rooms because the entire hotel is made of ice! Sometimes furs and animal skins are also provided for extra warmth. The ice hotel makes it clear to visitors that in some of the rooms they can expect to sleep in negative temperatures.

Features of Ice Hotels

Ice hotels, like other hotels, offer activities. The ice hotel in Canada offers fun events such as an ice slide, a snack shop, and a maze. Many ice hotels provide guided tours of the hotel. Some ice hotels have banquet rooms to host big events such as weddings.

Preparing for an Ice Hotel Stay

It is recommended to wear a lot of layers when going to any ice hotel, because some of the rooms are designed to be warmer than others. Many people who tour the ice hotels don't plan on staying overnight. Visiting an ice hotel would be an interesting, albeit chilly, experience!

   Nonfiction Reading Practice • EMC 3235 • © Evan-Moor Corp.

Name _____

Staying at an Ice Hotel

Fill in the circle by the correct answer. Then write the answers to numbers 3, 4, and 5.

1. One reason ice hotel visitors should wear a lot of layers is that _____.
   Ⓐ the ice hotel does not provide shelter
   Ⓑ temperatures can drop below zero
   Ⓒ they can stay in a warm room
   Ⓓ there are furs and animal skins on the beds

2. It would be most unlikely to find an ice hotel in _____.
   Ⓐ Australia
   Ⓑ Russia
   Ⓒ Switzerland
   Ⓓ Greenland

3. How does the Art Suite in the photo compare to a hotel room you've stayed in before?

   _____

   _____

4. Explain the purpose of putting a mattress and sleeping bags on the beds.

   _____

   _____

5. Would you rather stay in a traditional hotel or an ice hotel? Explain why.

   _____

   _____

Write About the Topic

Use the Writing Form to write about what you read.

How are ice hotels similar to other hotels you know about? How are they different? Use details from the text.

People Love Ice Hotels

Ice hotels are grand, majestic hotels made of ice. They accommodate guests in Sweden, Canada, Romania, Finland, and Norway. Although they are open for only a few months each year, they attract thousands of people from around the world.

Ice Hotel Basics

Ice hotels vary in terms of how many guest rooms they offer; some hotels might have 40 rooms, whereas others may have over 60. Although the hotels can be different, there are some basics that many ice hotels have. The beds are typically made of a large solid block of ice with a mattress placed on top. The hotel usually provides blankets, sleeping bags, and pillows to serve as a barrier between the ice and the sleeper's body. The rooms can get very cold (negative temperatures), so it is recommended that guests wear multiple layers of clothing. Ice hotels have banquet halls for large events such as weddings. They often have food and drink vendors. In a lot of ways, ice hotels function similarly to other hotels.

Ice bed with mattress and blankets

Lukas Maverick Greyson / Shutterstock.com

Building Ice Hotels

At the start of the cold winter season, people arrive on location to help build the ice hotel. The hotel in Sweden, for example, is built by over 100 artists. It's usually built to cover the same area of land every year, about 60,000 square feet (5,500 square meters). The artists use tons of ice and another material called "snice." Snice gets its name from "snow" and "ice" because the way it freezes gives it characteristics that are in between snow and ice. It's denser than typical snow, so it melts more slowly and provides excellent insulation for the hotel. This helps prevent the inside of the hotel from melting quickly.

Ice Hotel Attractions

The ice hotel in Sweden attracts about 50,000 to 60,000 visitors every year. Many people plan weddings at ice hotels. The hotels offer activities that guests can enjoy in addition to the rooms and suites. Visitors can do hikes and food tastings, go rafting, and take ice sculpting classes. The ice hotel itself lasts for only four months. But its guests come from all over the world in that short period of time. The ice hotel in Sweden accepts guests and offers activities all year round, but it's only during winter that the ice building is available to sleep in.

Inside an ice structure

Jorg Hackemann / Shutterstock.com

Nonfiction Reading Practice • EMC 3235 • © Evan-Moor Corp.

Name _____

People Love Ice Hotels

Fill in the circle by the correct answer. Then write the answers to numbers 3, 4, and 5.

1. Ice hotels are similar to traditional hotels because they both usually _____.
   - Ⓐ have snice in their buildings
   - Ⓑ stay open for only a few months every year
   - Ⓒ require multiple layers of clothing
   - Ⓓ offer beds, food, and entertainment

2. Which detail supports the idea that ice hotels are beautiful?
   - Ⓐ The rooms can get very cold.
   - Ⓑ They are built by artists.
   - Ⓒ There are food and drink vendors.
   - Ⓓ One of them has an area of 60,000 square feet (5,500 square meters).

3. Could an ice hotel be successful without snice? Explain why or why not.

   _____

   _____

4. Why would someone choose to host a large event at an ice hotel?

   _____

   _____

5. What can you infer about ice hotels from the fact that they attract so many guests?

   _____

   _____

Write About the Topic

Use the Writing Form to write about what you read.

> Write a short essay persuading a friend that it would be safe and fun to stay at an ice hotel. Use details from the text.

Ice Hotel: A Modern Symbol

Have you ever thought about staying in an ice hotel? There are ice hotels in Sweden, Canada, Finland, Norway, and Romania. Ice hotels have existed for only a few decades, yet they are very popular tourist destinations. With their great beauty and all they have to offer, one can't help but view these icy buildings as symbols. They are symbols of what modern travelers value.

Archway in an ice hotel

ihorga / Shutterstock.com

Dependability and Comfort

Ice hotels are made of ice, snow, and "snice," a dense material that has characteristics of both snow and ice. The hotels are built at the start of winter. Snice keeps the hotel insulated so well that the inside remains solid for at least 3–4 months. The archways, walls, ceilings, tables, doors, and beds are made of solid ice. The beds have added comfort from pillows, mattresses, and sleeping bags that the hotels provide. Suites tend to be bigger, with bathrooms, saunas, and lounges.

Jorg Hackemann / Shutterstock.com

Ice hotel room with beds and thick blankets

Beauty and Innovation

Many artists join the ice hotel building teams each winter. The hotels offer a range of rooms and suites. The hotel in Sweden has Art Suites. These are hand-carved rooms with detailed ice sculptures, tables, and doors. The Art Suites are among the most expensive rooms at the ice hotel, but the entire hotel is beautiful. Archways and hallways are lit up with colorful fluorescent lights, creating a dreamy effect. Even the outside of the hotel looks icy and magical. Technology plays a role in making the hotel look edgy and modern each year.

Adventure, Entertainment, and Variety

When visiting an ice hotel, guests have a chance to sleep in a room that reaches below-freezing temperatures. They can travel through ice mazes, slip on ice slides, take ice sculpting courses, go on hikes, and so much more.

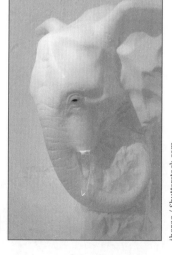

Ice sculpture in the ice hotel in Sweden

ihorga / Shutterstock.com

Nonfiction Reading Practice • EMC 3235 • © Evan-Moor Corp.

Ice Hotel: A Modern Symbol

Fill in the circle by the correct answer. Then write the answers to numbers 3, 4, and 5.

1. The main idea of this text is that ice hotels symbolize _____.
   - Ⓐ the values of the countries they are built in
   - Ⓑ how travelers should behave
   - Ⓒ an excellent modern traveling experience
   - Ⓓ the strengths and weaknesses of hotels

2. The bold headings in the text indicate _____, according to the author.
   - Ⓐ traits that people find only in ice hotels
   - Ⓑ things that people are trying to avoid
   - Ⓒ what Sweden, Canada, Finland, Norway, and Romania are known for
   - Ⓓ things that modern travelers value

3. Ice hotels have become popular in a short time. What does this suggest about them?

   _____

   _____

4. Is it significant that artists help build ice hotels? Explain why or why not.

   _____

   _____

5. Do you think the author would stay in an ice hotel? Explain why or why not.

   _____

   _____

Write About the Topic

Use the Writing Form to write about what you read.

Is the author's claim that ice hotels symbolize what modern travelers value convincing? Use details from the text for support.

Idea Map

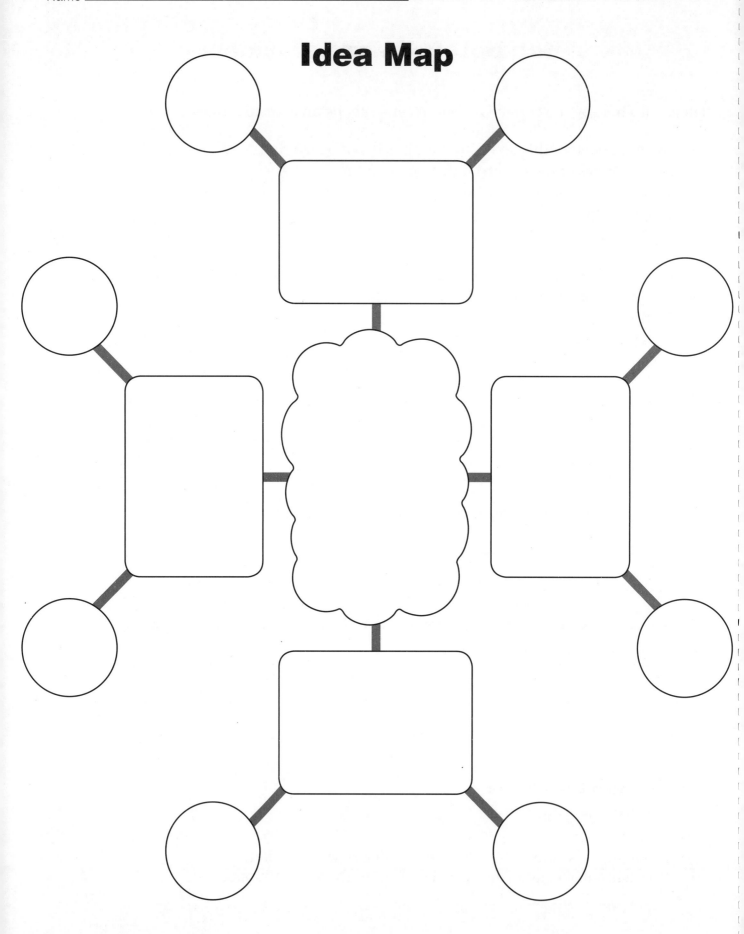

Nonfiction Reading Practice • EMC 3235 • © Evan-Moor Corp.

All About It

Topic

[ ]

Details

Who: _____

What: _____

When: _____

Where: _____

Why: _____

How: _____

Name _____

Same or Different?

Both

1. _____

2. _____

Same or Different?

Name _____

Argument or Opinion Chart

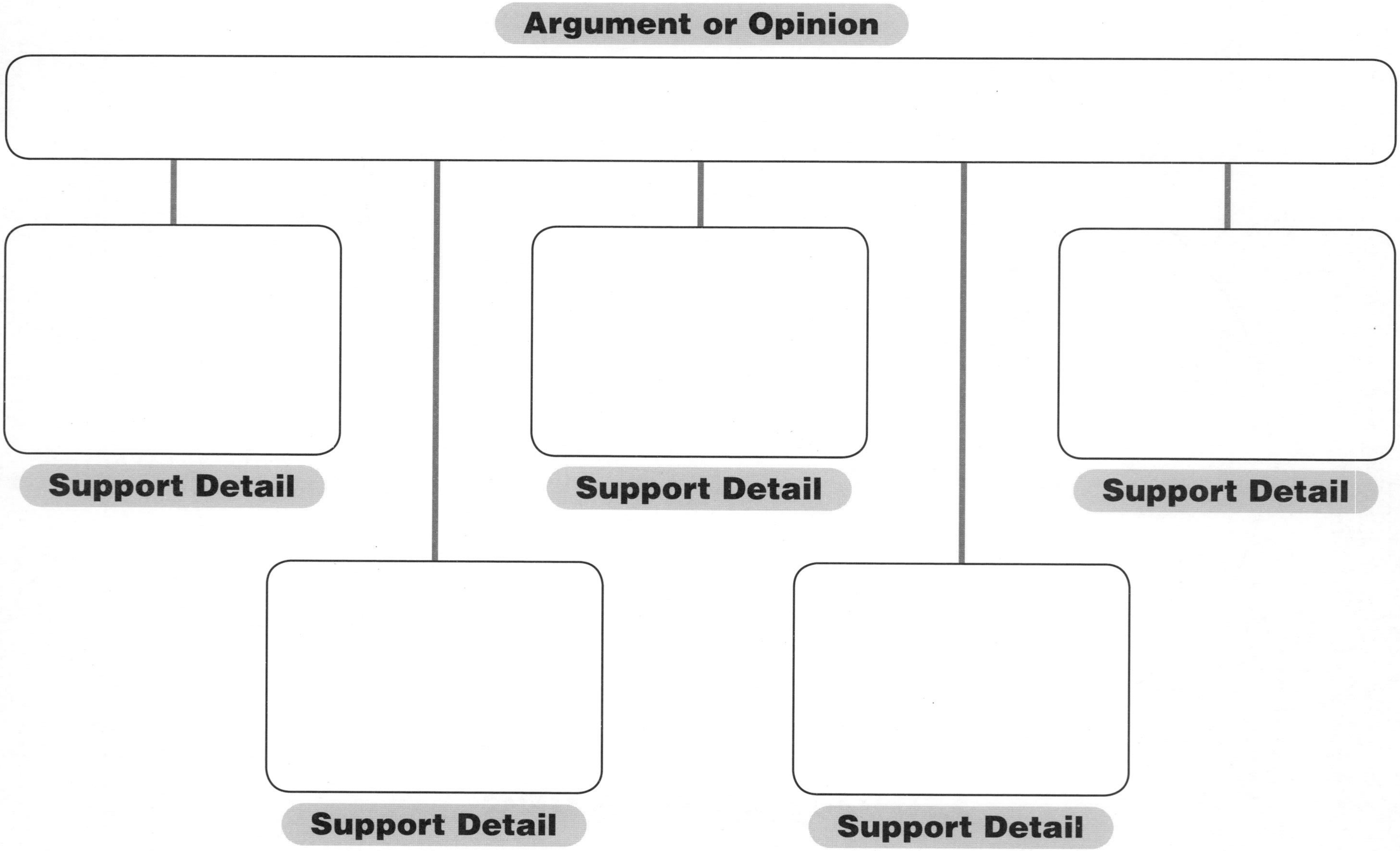

Argument or Opinion

Support Detail

Support Detail

Support Detail

Support Detail

Support Detail

Support Detail

Cause and Effect Chart

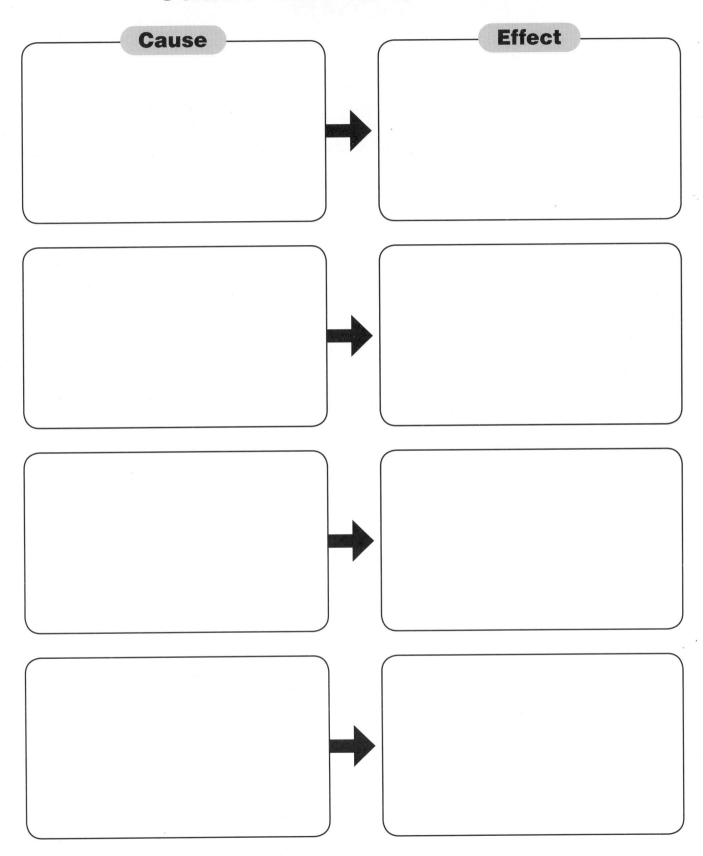

Cause   **Effect**

Graphic Organizer 185

Name _____

T-Chart

My writing topic: _____

Before	After

Answer Key

Page 15

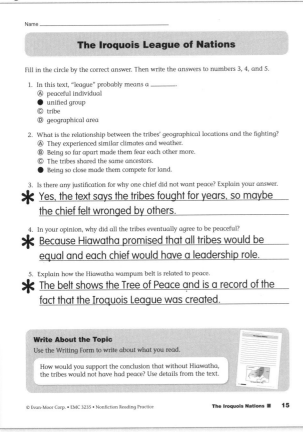

Name _____

The Iroquois League of Nations

Fill in the circle by the correct answer. Then write the answers to numbers 3, 4, and 5.

1. In this text, "league" probably means a _____
   Ⓐ peaceful individual
   ● unified group
   Ⓒ tribe
   Ⓓ geographical area

2. What is the relationship between the tribes' geographical locations and the fighting?
   Ⓐ They experienced similar climates and weather.
   Ⓑ Being so far apart made them fear each other more.
   Ⓒ The tribes shared the same ancestors.
   ● Being so close made them compete for land.

3. Is there any justification for why one chief did not want peace? Explain your answer.
   ※ Yes, the text says the tribes fought for years, so maybe the chief felt wronged by others.

4. In your opinion, why did all the tribes eventually agree to be peaceful?
   ※ Because Hiawatha promised that all tribes would be equal and each chief would have a leadership role.

5. Explain how the Hiawatha wampum belt is related to peace.
   ※ The belt shows the Tree of Peace and is a record of the fact that the Iroquois League was created.

Write About the Topic
Use the Writing Form to write about what you read.

How would you support the conclusion that without Hiawatha, the tribes would not have had peace? Use details from the text.

© Evan-Moor Corp. • EMC 3235 • Nonfiction Reading Practice   **The Iroquois Nations** ■   15

Page 17

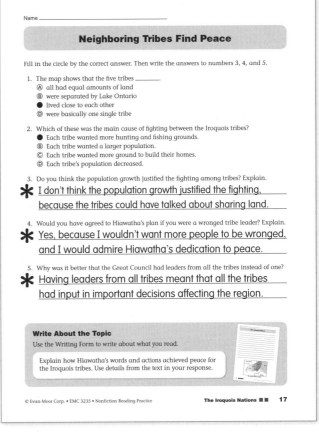

Name _____

Neighboring Tribes Find Peace

Fill in the circle by the correct answer. Then write the answers to numbers 3, 4, and 5.

1. The map shows that the five tribes _____
   Ⓐ all had equal amounts of land
   Ⓑ were separated by Lake Ontario
   ● lived close to each other
   Ⓓ were basically one single tribe

2. Which of these was the main cause of fighting between the Iroquois tribes?
   ● Each tribe wanted more hunting and fishing grounds.
   Ⓑ Each tribe wanted a larger population.
   Ⓒ Each tribe wanted more ground to build their homes.
   Ⓓ Each tribe's population decreased.

3. Do you think the population growth justified the fighting among tribes? Explain.
   ※ I don't think the population growth justified the fighting, because the tribes could have talked about sharing land.

4. Would you have agreed to Hiawatha's plan if you were a wronged tribe leader? Explain.
   ※ Yes, because I wouldn't want more people to be wronged, and I would admire Hiawatha's dedication to peace.

5. Why was it better that the Great Council had leaders from all the tribes instead of one?
   ※ Having leaders from all tribes meant that all the tribes had input in important decisions affecting the region.

Write About the Topic
Use the Writing Form to write about what you read.

Explain how Hiawatha's words and actions achieved peace for the Iroquois tribes. Use details from the text in your response.

© Evan-Moor Corp. • EMC 3235 • Nonfiction Reading Practice   **The Iroquois Nations** ■ ■   17

Page 19

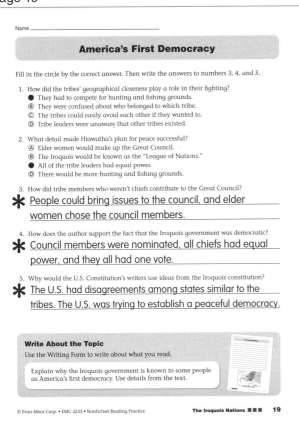

Name _____

America's First Democracy

Fill in the circle by the correct answer. Then write the answers to numbers 3, 4, and 5.

1. How did the tribes' geographical closeness play a role in their fighting?
   ● They had to compete for hunting and fishing grounds.
   Ⓑ They were confused about who belonged to which tribe.
   Ⓒ The tribes could easily avoid each other if they wanted to.
   Ⓓ Tribe leaders were unaware that other tribes existed.

2. What detail made Hiawatha's plan for peace successful?
   Ⓐ Elder women would make up the Great Council.
   Ⓑ The Iroquois would be known as the "League of Nations."
   ● All of the tribe leaders had equal power.
   Ⓓ There would be more hunting and fishing grounds.

3. How did tribe members who weren't chiefs contribute to the Great Council?
   ※ People could bring issues to the council, and elder women chose the council members.

4. How does the author support the fact that the Iroquois government was democratic?
   ※ Council members were nominated, all chiefs had equal power, and they all had one vote.

5. Why would the U.S. Constitution's writers use ideas from the Iroquois constitution?
   ※ The U.S. had disagreements among states similar to the tribes. The U.S. was trying to establish a peaceful democracy.

Write About the Topic
Use the Writing Form to write about what you read.

Explain why the Iroquois government is known to some people as America's first democracy. Use details from the text.

© Evan-Moor Corp. • EMC 3235 • Nonfiction Reading Practice   **The Iroquois Nations** ■ ■ ■   19

Page 25

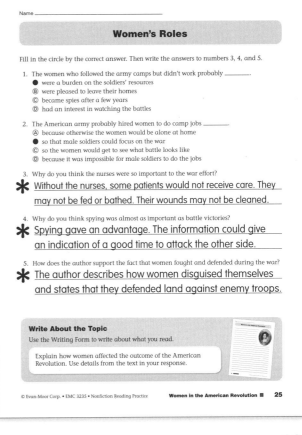

Name _____

Women's Roles

Fill in the circle by the correct answer. Then write the answers to numbers 3, 4, and 5.

1. The women who followed the army camps but didn't work probably _____
   ● were a burden on the soldiers' resources
   Ⓑ were pleased to leave their homes
   Ⓒ became spies after a few years
   Ⓓ had an interest in watching the battles

2. The American army probably hired women to do camp jobs _____
   Ⓐ because otherwise the women would be alone at home
   ● so that male soldiers could focus on the war
   Ⓒ so the women would get to see what battle looks like
   Ⓓ because it was impossible for male soldiers to do the jobs

3. Why do you think the nurses were so important to the war effort?
   ※ Without the nurses, some patients would not receive care. They may not be fed or bathed. Their wounds may not be cleaned.

4. Why do you think spying was almost as important as battle victories?
   ※ Spying gave an advantage. The information could give an indication of a good time to attack the other side.

5. How does the author support the fact that women fought and defended during the war?
   ※ The author describes how women disguised themselves and states that they defended land against enemy troops.

Write About the Topic
Use the Writing Form to write about what you read.

Explain how women affected the outcome of the American Revolution. Use details from the text in your response.

© Evan-Moor Corp. • EMC 3235 • Nonfiction Reading Practice   **Women in the American Revolution** ■   25

These answers will vary. Examples given.

Page 27

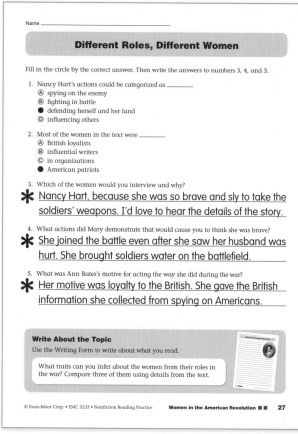

Name _____

Different Roles, Different Women

Fill in the circle by the correct answer. Then write the answers to numbers 3, 4, and 5.

1. Nancy Hart's actions could be categorized as _____.
   - Ⓐ spying on the enemy
   - Ⓑ fighting in battle
   - ● defending herself and her land
   - Ⓓ influencing others

2. Most of the women in the text were _____.
   - Ⓐ British loyalists
   - Ⓑ influential writers
   - Ⓒ in organizations
   - ● American patriots

3. Which of the women would you interview and why?
   ✱ Nancy Hart, because she was so brave and sly to take the soldiers' weapons. I'd love to hear the details of the story.

4. What actions did Mary demonstrate that would cause you to think she was brave?
   ✱ She joined the battle even after she saw her husband was hurt. She brought soldiers water on the battlefield.

5. What was Ann Bates's motive for acting the way she did during the war?
   ✱ Her motive was loyalty to the British. She gave the British information she collected from spying on Americans.

Write About the Topic
Use the Writing Form to write about what you read.

What traits can you infer about the women from their roles in the war? Compare three of them using details from the text.

© Evan-Moor Corp. • EMC 3235 • Nonfiction Reading Practice **Women in the American Revolution** ■ ■ 27

Page 29

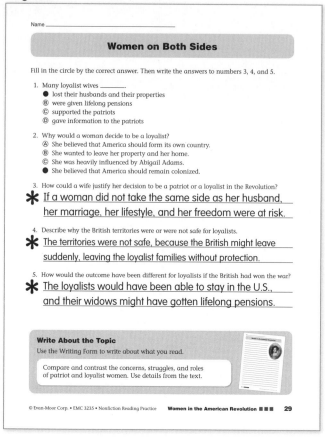

Name _____

Women on Both Sides

Fill in the circle by the correct answer. Then write the answers to numbers 3, 4, and 5.

1. Many loyalist wives _____.
   - ● lost their husbands and their properties
   - Ⓑ were given lifelong pensions
   - Ⓒ supported the patriots
   - Ⓓ gave information to the patriots

2. Why would a woman decide to be a loyalist?
   - Ⓐ She believed that America should form its own country.
   - Ⓑ She wanted to leave her property and her home.
   - Ⓒ She was heavily influenced by Abigail Adams.
   - ● She believed that America should remain colonized.

3. How could a wife justify her decision to be a patriot or a loyalist in the Revolution?
   ✱ If a woman did not take the same side as her husband, her marriage, her lifestyle, and her freedom were at risk.

4. Describe why the British territories were or were not safe for loyalists.
   ✱ The territories were not safe, because the British might leave suddenly, leaving the loyalist families without protection.

5. How would the outcome have been different for loyalists if the British had won the war?
   ✱ The loyalists would have been able to stay in the U.S., and their widows might have gotten lifelong pensions.

Write About the Topic
Use the Writing Form to write about what you read.

Compare and contrast the concerns, struggles, and roles of patriot and loyalist women. Use details from the text.

© Evan-Moor Corp. • EMC 3235 • Nonfiction Reading Practice **Women in the American Revolution** ■ ■ ■ 29

Page 35

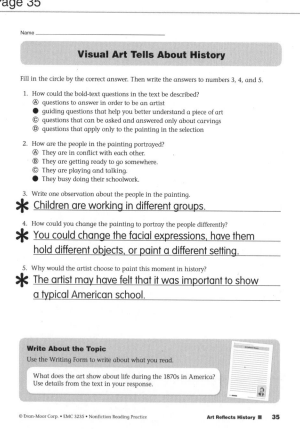

Name _____

Visual Art Tells About History

Fill in the circle by the correct answer. Then write the answers to numbers 3, 4, and 5.

1. How could the bold-text questions in the text be described?
   - Ⓐ questions to answer in order to be an artist
   - ● guiding questions that help you better understand a piece of art
   - Ⓒ questions that can be asked and answered only about carvings
   - Ⓓ questions that apply only to the painting in the selection

2. How are the people in the painting portrayed?
   - Ⓐ They are in conflict with each other.
   - Ⓑ They are getting ready to go somewhere.
   - Ⓒ They are playing and talking.
   - ● They busy doing their schoolwork.

3. Write one observation about the people in the painting.
   ✱ Children are working in different groups.

4. How could you change the painting to portray the people differently?
   ✱ You could change the facial expressions, have them hold different objects, or paint a different setting.

5. Why would the artist choose to paint this moment in history?
   ✱ The artist may have felt that it was important to show a typical American school.

Write About the Topic
Use the Writing Form to write about what you read.

What does the art show about life during the 1870s in America? Use details from the text in your response.

© Evan-Moor Corp. • EMC 3235 • Nonfiction Reading Practice **Art Reflects History** ■ 35

Page 37

Name _____

Music Tells About History

Fill in the circle by the correct answer. Then write the answers to numbers 3, 4, and 5.

1. Why does the singer mention pilgrims in "My Country 'Tis of Thee"?
   - Ⓐ The song is about how the pilgrims came to America.
   - Ⓑ The song is about the area where the pilgrims lived.
   - ● The pilgrims played an important role in America's history.
   - Ⓓ Samuel F. Smith was a pilgrim.

2. "This Land Is Your Land" mentions specific places in the U.S. to _____.
   - ● show that the entire country is free, from coast to coast
   - Ⓑ provide geographical information in the song
   - Ⓒ inform listeners of how far he has traveled
   - Ⓓ make the song appeal to people in different areas

3. In Guthrie's song, why does the singer claim that the "other" side is for you and me?
   ✱ The singer values freedom. The singer wants to be on the free side of the "No Trespassing" sign.

4. What details do the songs give us about the geography of the United States of America? Are these details an important part of the songs?
   ✱ The song lyrics talk about hills, mountains, forests, and waters. The details are important because they tell people about the U.S.

5. What things do Americans probably value most, according to these songs?
   ✱ Americans value their freedom and liberty, their history, their forefathers, and their beautiful lands.

Write About the Topic
Use the Writing Form to write about what you read.

Compare and contrast the themes in the two songs. Use examples from the text to support your statements.

© Evan-Moor Corp. • EMC 3235 • Nonfiction Reading Practice **Art Reflects History** ■ ■ 37

✻ **These answers will vary. Examples given.**

Page 39

Name _____

Literature Tells About History

Fill in the circle by the correct answer. Then write the answers to numbers 3, 4, and 5.

1. What inference can you make about Mark Twain as an author?
   Ⓐ He is against slavery.
   Ⓑ He wishes he were a boy again.
   Ⓒ He felt it was important to write about criminals.
   ● He felt it was important to write about life in the South during slavery.

2. *The Adventures of Tom Sawyer* reflects reality by focusing on _____.
   Ⓐ an American family's ideal life
   ● hardship and moral struggles
   Ⓒ the life of emancipated people
   Ⓓ the Reconstruction period

3. In your own words, explain what realism is in literature.
   ✻ It is when authors want to write a story that reflects the real world as it is, including bad things.

4. How does the text support the idea that the Civil War caused new issues in the country?
   ✻ The text mentions examples such as freed people needing jobs and the South's devastated economy.

5. Would you recommend a fictional book from the 1870s to someone who wants to learn more about American history? Explain why or why not.
   ✻ Yes, because even a fictional story may tell about how life was back then because realism was popular.

Write About the Topic
Use the Writing Form to write about what you read.

Describe the relationship between realism, the Reconstruction period, and *The Adventures of Tom Sawyer*. Use examples.

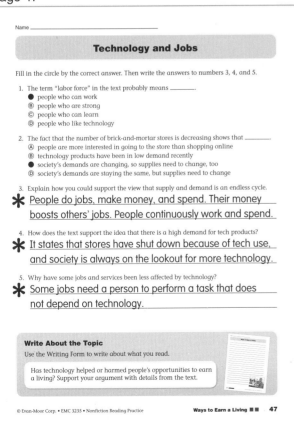

© Evan-Moor Corp. • EMC 3235 • Nonfiction Reading Practice　　　Art Reflects History ▪ ▪ ▪　**39**

Page 45

Name _____

The Basics of Earning a Living

Fill in the circle by the correct answer. Then write the answers to numbers 3, 4, and 5.

1. Why would a job be "geographically limited" to a specific area?
   ● The job requires a specific geographical landscape or region.
   Ⓑ The person doing the job needs to have specific skills.
   Ⓒ The good or service provided requires only U.S. dollars.
   Ⓓ The job is in demand everywhere.

2. The word "robust" probably means "_____."
   Ⓐ weak
   ● strong
   Ⓒ special
   Ⓓ complicated

3. Explain two aspects of a healthy economy.
   ✻ A healthy economy has a demand for goods and services and an ability to supply those goods and services.

4. List some jobs you know of that are not in the chart and are limited geographically.
   ✻ A ship captain, a forest ranger, a surfing instructor

5. How do goods and services boost the economy?
   ✻ Goods and services depend on jobs. People do jobs, make money, and spend on goods and services.

Write About the Topic
Use the Writing Form to write about what you read.

Choose one occupation in the chart that is geographically limited and one that is universal. Explain why this is so.

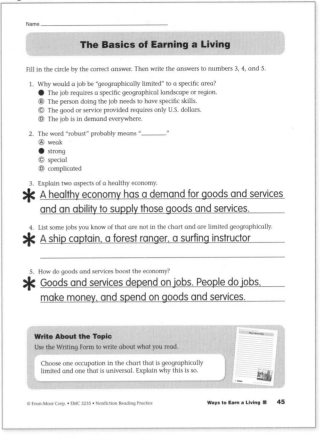

© Evan-Moor Corp. • EMC 3235 • Nonfiction Reading Practice　　　Ways to Earn a Living ▪　**45**

Page 47

Name _____

Technology and Jobs

Fill in the circle by the correct answer. Then write the answers to numbers 3, 4, and 5.

1. The term "labor force" in the text probably means _____.
   ● people who can work
   Ⓑ people who are strong
   Ⓒ people who can learn
   Ⓓ people who like technology

2. The fact that the number of brick-and-mortar stores is decreasing shows that _____.
   Ⓐ people are more interested in going to the store than shopping online
   Ⓑ technology products have been in low demand recently
   ● society's demands are changing, so supplies need to change, too
   Ⓓ society's demands are staying the same, but supplies need to change

3. Explain how you could support the view that supply and demand is an endless cycle.
   ✻ People do jobs, make money, and spend. Their money boosts others' jobs. People continuously work and spend.

4. How does the text support the idea that there is a high demand for tech products?
   ✻ It states that stores have shut down because of tech use, and society is always on the lookout for more technology.

5. Why have some jobs and services been less affected by technology?
   ✻ Some jobs need a person to perform a task that does not depend on technology.

Write About the Topic
Use the Writing Form to write about what you read.

Has technology helped or harmed people's opportunities to earn a living? Support your argument with details from the text.

© Evan-Moor Corp. • EMC 3235 • Nonfiction Reading Practice　　　Ways to Earn a Living ▪ ▪　**47**

Page 49

Name _____

Creating New Jobs

Fill in the circle by the correct answer. Then write the answers to numbers 3, 4, and 5.

1. From the chart, you can make the inference that _____.
   Ⓐ switchboard operators are now doing their jobs for mobile calls
   Ⓑ long-distance calls are no longer being made on landline phones
   ● switchboards aren't necessary to make long-distance calls now
   Ⓓ the U.S. no longer has a need for phones of any kind

2. How can we estimate what the world population will be in 2050?
   Ⓐ We know what the current world population is.
   Ⓑ There is data from 2050 that informs us of the population.
   Ⓒ We can assume that the population will not grow very much.
   ● We can estimate based on the growth rate from recent decades.

3. Explain why jobs change when demand changes.
   ✻ Jobs are based on what people need or want. When demand changes, a job is created to meet the demand.

4. How does population growth affect the kinds of jobs that are needed?
   ✻ Population growth affects jobs because a greater number of people using something creates a greater demand for it.

5. Based on the chart, what's so different about the types of jobs in 1950 and 2017?
   ✻ Jobs in 1950 involved more manual work, like delivering milk or setting up pins. Jobs in 2017 use technology.

Write About the Topic
Use the Writing Form to write about what you read.

Explain how jobs will be different 60 years from now and why, and predict what some future jobs will be. Use text details.

© Evan-Moor Corp. • EMC 3235 • Nonfiction Reading Practice　　　Ways to Earn a Living ▪ ▪ ▪　**49**

© Evan-Moor Corp. • EMC 3235 • Nonfiction Reading Practice

✳ These answers will vary. Examples given.

Page 55

Name _____

The Water Cycle

Fill in the circle by the correct answer. Then write the answers to numbers 3, 4, and 5.

1. One of the main ideas in the text is that _____.
   - Ⓐ precipitation can be rain, snow, hail, or sleet
   - Ⓑ we drink the same water today that dinosaurs drank
   - Ⓒ condensation follows the evaporation stage
   - ● all stages of the water cycle are equally important

2. How is evaporation similar to condensation?
   - ● In both stages water changes its form.
   - Ⓑ Both stages involve rain and clouds.
   - Ⓒ They are more important than precipitation.
   - Ⓓ In both stages, the ocean plays an important role.

3. Why is the precipitation stage needed for the water cycle to work?

   ✳ The other stages could not happen without precipitation. There would be no water to evaporate.

4. Explain how the diagram helped you understand the water cycle.

   ✳ The diagram gives an idea of what the water cycle looks like in action in nature.

5. What do you think would happen if the water cycle stopped working?

   ✳ Earth would slowly run out of water; plants would start drying up; we wouldn't have water to drink.

Write About the Topic
Use the Writing Form to write about what you read.

Write about the water cycle. Describe what it is and how it works. Use details from the text in your description.

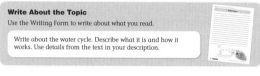

© Evan-Moor Corp. • EMC 3235 • Nonfiction Reading Practice   Earth's Water ■ **55**

Page 57

Name _____

Earth's Limited Fresh Water

Fill in the circle by the correct answer. Then write the answers to numbers 3, 4, and 5.

1. Why is it important that more than 96% of Earth's water is salt water?
   - Ⓐ This fact shows how many marine animals depend on salt water.
   - Ⓑ It shows that humans, animals, and plants are able to use most of Earth's water for survival.
   - Ⓒ We do not have to be concerned at all about water pollution in salt water.
   - ● It means that we can't use most of Earth's water for survival.

2. What inference can be made about polluted water?
   - Ⓐ It smells bad but is probably safe to drink.
   - ● Drinking it could harm people and animals.
   - Ⓒ The water cycle is a solution for polluted water.
   - Ⓓ It is found only in wells and springs.

3. Would it be better if fresh water did not evaporate? Explain why or why not.

   ✳ It wouldn't be better, because the stages of the water cycle refresh water and keep it usable and clean.

4. Write a main idea from the text and a detail that supports it.

   ✳ Main idea: Earth's fresh water is limited. Detail: Most of it is in glaciers and polar ice caps, where we can't get it.

5. Explain what water overuse is and why it's a problem.

   ✳ It is when people waste water or use it for purposes that aren't necessary. It limits our freshwater supply.

Write About the Topic
Use the Writing Form to write about what you read.

Explain the relationship between the water cycle and Earth's supply of fresh water. Use details from the text in your explanation.

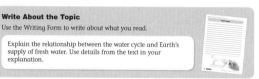

© Evan-Moor Corp. • EMC 3235 • Nonfiction Reading Practice   Earth's Water ■ ■ **57**

Page 59

Name _____

Conserving Fresh Water

Fill in the circle by the correct answer. Then write the answers to numbers 3, 4, and 5.

1. According to the pie chart, _____.
   - Ⓐ leaks cause the heaviest use of water in typical homes
   - Ⓑ very few American homes use water for flushing the toilet
   - ● we know how more than 90% of water is used every day
   - Ⓓ we get most of our household water from precipitation

2. How can the information in the pie chart help us to conserve water?
   - ● The chart can make people aware of how much water they use or overuse.
   - Ⓑ We can see that clothes washers should be banned.
   - Ⓒ The chart shows specific houses that overuse water.
   - Ⓓ We can use the information to increase the supply of fresh water.

3. What steps would you recommend to people who want to conserve water?

   ✳ Turn off the faucet as much as possible, be mindful of water use, and fix leaks.

4. Explain how the author uses each paragraph to support each bold-text main idea.

   ✳ The author uses facts and gives reasons for why the bold main idea is true. The author includes a percentage.

5. Why can't we rely on the water cycle alone to have enough fresh water?

   ✳ The human population is increasing, limiting our water supply even more. There are other threats to water, too.

Write About the Topic
Use the Writing Form to write about what you read.

Did the author succeed at proving that water conservation is necessary? Write an argument for why or why not. Use examples.

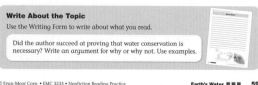

© Evan-Moor Corp. • EMC 3235 • Nonfiction Reading Practice   Earth's Water ■ ■ ■ **59**

Page 65

Name _____

The Basics of Matter

Fill in the circle by the correct answer. Then write the answers to numbers 3, 4, and 5.

1. Earth has the same amount of water as it did billions of years ago because _____.
   - Ⓐ water only moves within the ocean
   - Ⓑ water does not have a mass, so it's not as heavy
   - Ⓒ even invisible things such as air are made of matter
   - ● of the law of conservation of mass

2. _____ is an example of a chemical reaction.
   - Ⓐ Water changing into ice
   - ● An egg becoming hard-boiled
   - Ⓒ A frying pan heating up
   - Ⓓ Folding a dollar bill

3. If the person had eaten the orange peel, too, would the mass in the room have changed? Explain why or why not.

   No. The orange's atoms still would have been in the room, just rearranged.

4. Does the state of matter in an object affect the mass? Explain why or why not.

   No. The state of matter does not affect the amount of matter. Even if the state changes, the amount is the same.

5. When substances combine or break apart, what is happening to the matter?

   ✳ The matter is being rearranged, which means it is moving and changing.

Write About the Topic
Use the Writing Form to write about what you read.

Explain how the law of conservation of mass relates to matter as it moves through the water cycle. Use details and examples.

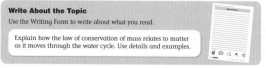

© Evan-Moor Corp. • EMC 3235 • Nonfiction Reading Practice   Matter and Mass ■ **65**

Page 67

Name _____

Law of Conservation of Mass

Fill in the circle by the correct answer. Then write the answers to numbers 3, 4, and 5.

1. When a living thing digests food, the _____.
   Ⓐ chemical reaction does not occur
   ● food's matter is rearranged
   Ⓒ living thing's matter is rearranged
   Ⓓ law of conservation of mass doesn't apply

2. When a landform or a living thing gets smaller, it's because _____.
   Ⓐ new matter formed in another place
   Ⓑ Earth's mass decreased
   Ⓒ matter was used up and disappeared
   ● matter was transferred from it to another place

3. What do microorganisms have in common with erosion?
   ✳ They are both important in Earth's natural cycles.
   They break down matter so that it can be rearranged.

4. Explain how the law of conservation of mass allows Earth's cycles to continue.
   ✳ The law ensures that Earth will never run out of matter,
   so water, organic matter, and rock will always rearrange.

5. How are humans and their belongings subject to the law of conservation of mass?
   ✳ Humans grow, gain and lose weight, and use energy.
   The properties of our matter, like the color of our house,
   can change.

Write About the Topic
Use the Writing Form to write about what you read.

Elaborate on why Earth's total mass will never change. Use details from the text, and provide your own examples.

Page 69

Name _____

Matter in Natural Cycles

Fill in the circle by the correct answer. Then write the answers to numbers 3, 4, and 5.

1. An organism growing bigger is evidence that _____.
   Ⓐ energy that didn't exist on Earth before has transferred to the organism
   Ⓑ the organism has created matter that didn't exist before
   ● matter has transferred to the organism from another place
   Ⓓ the organism has not gained or lost any mass

2. According to the text, _____.
   ● the matter in sedimentary rock eventually transfers to another place
   Ⓑ igneous rock cannot break down as other rocks can
   Ⓒ weathering and erosion is the only way rock matter changes
   Ⓓ sedimentary rock is not composed of matter

3. Explain how the law of conservation of mass makes it possible for the grasshopper to help the frog survive.
   ✳ The matter in the grasshopper's body will break down
   inside the frog, and its energy will transfer to the frog.

4. What would happen if food matter simply disappeared after organisms ate? Explain how Earth would be different.
   ✳ Life on Earth would not have existed this long, because
   matter would not get passed along. It could run out.

5. Why is the law of conservation of mass essential for all of the natural cycles to work?
   ✳ The reason these processes are cycles is because they
   are ongoing due to the law. All of the cycles need matter.

Write About the Topic
Use the Writing Form to write about what you read.

Compare and contrast how matter moves through the three cycles mentioned in the text. Use details and examples.

Page 75

Name _____

Ecosystem Relationships

Fill in the circle by the correct answer. Then write the answers to numbers 3, 4, and 5.

1. In the second photo within the text, the _____.
   Ⓐ tree is benefitted by the fungus's living cells
   ● fungus is surviving from the tree's living cells
   Ⓒ fungus is growing on the tree, but the tree is unharmed
   Ⓓ tree and the fungus are sharing a mutualistic relationship

2. When birds follow cattle to find bugs to eat, the disturbed bugs are _____.
   Ⓐ benefitted
   Ⓑ parasitic
   Ⓒ predators
   ● prey

3. What would happen if the tree in a tree-fungi parasitic relationship suddenly died? Explain why this would happen.
   The fungi would die because they depend on the tree's
   living cells to survive.

4. In your opinion, which is the worst kind of relationship for an organism? Explain why.
   ✳ If you are the prey, a predation relationship is the worst.

5. Would it be possible for an organism not to be part of an ecosystem relationship? Why or why not?
   ✳ No, all organisms must eat (whether plants or animals).
   All organisms must compete for resources.

Write About the Topic
Use the Writing Form to write about what you read.

Describe an ecosystem you studied or know about and identify relationships from the text that are in it. Give specific examples.

Page 77

Name _____

Making Ecosystem Connections

Fill in the circle by the correct answer. Then write the answers to numbers 3, 4, and 5.

1. Which sentence describes a mutualistic relationship?
   ● Bees use flowers for pollen to make nectar, and flowers use bees to reproduce.
   Ⓑ Vultures and hyenas compete for carrion as a food source in the savanna.
   Ⓒ Mosquitos land on animals and feed on their blood for nutrients.
   Ⓓ Rattle, an herb, attaches to grass roots and takes nutrients away from the grass.

2. Which of the following animals can be prey, according to the text?
   Ⓐ jackal
   Ⓑ eagle
   ● meerkat
   Ⓓ vulture

3. What would happen if two species were in competition, and one was more successful?
   ✳ The successful species would thrive, and its population
   would grow. The other species would decrease or die off.

4. Is ecosystem balance important? How could eagles affect the mouse population?
   ✳ Balance is important. If eagles ate too many meerkats,
   the mouse population would increase.

5. Explain what it means for a species to be "benefitted" or "harmed" in an ecosystem.
   ✳ A benefit helps a species' population grow and survive.
   A species is harmed when it is hurt, killed, or made weak.

Write About the Topic
Use the Writing Form to write about what you read.

Compare the roles that the meerkat and the rhino play in their relationships with other species. Use details from the text.

Page 79

Name _____

Ecosystem Balance

Fill in the circle by the correct answer. Then write the answers to numbers 3, 4, and 5.

1. According to the diagram, _____.
   - Ⓐ giraffes have no predators
   - Ⓑ lions feed on their own species
   - Ⓒ cheetahs and rhinoceroses compete with each other
   - ⬤ giraffes and elephants compete with each other

2. The last paragraph of the text provides questions that _____.
   - Ⓐ the author and readers should know the exact answers to
   - ⬤ encourage thinking about an organism's role in its ecosystem
   - Ⓒ are related to a situation that is absolutely impossible
   - Ⓓ are meant to make the reader think mainly about parasitism

3. Explain why predation and competition are not considered symbiosis.

✳ Predation requires one species to die, not survive. And species that compete probably don't need each other.

4. What would happen if only one species at the top of the food chain were to disappear?

✳ Either the population of the species that the predator fed on would grow, or its competitors would grow.

5. According to the diagram, which animals are in competition with each other?

✳ The cheetah, panther, and lion compete for prey. The elephant and giraffe compete for plant food.

Write About the Topic

Use the Writing Form to write about what you read.

Write about why the balance of different species in an ecosystem is important. Use details and examples.

© Evan-Moor Corp. • EMC 3235 • Nonfiction Reading Practice   Relationships in Nature ▪▪▪   79

Page 85

Name _____

What Are Stars?

Fill in the circle by the correct answer. Then write the answers to numbers 3, 4, and 5.

1. According to the text, stars _____.
   - ⬤ range in size and in distance from Earth
   - Ⓑ are all the same distance from Earth
   - Ⓒ are all the same size and temperature
   - Ⓓ can be seen only with a telescope

2. The diagram shows that electromagnetic radiation _____.
   - Ⓐ is everywhere we go
   - Ⓑ is always visible
   - Ⓒ moves in a straight line
   - ⬤ moves in waves

3. Explain what the sun is composed of.

✳ The sun is made of hot gases, mostly hydrogen and helium.

4. What effect does the distance from Earth have on how stars appear to us?

✳ Stars that are farther away seem smaller and not as bright. Closer stars seem brighter.

5. Explain which forms of electromagnetic radiation you are familiar with and how.

✳ I use sunglasses to protect my eyes from ultraviolet radiation. I know about radio waves.

Write About the Topic

Use the Writing Form to write about what you read.

Compare and contrast the sun in our solar system to the other stars in the galaxy. Use details and examples from the text.

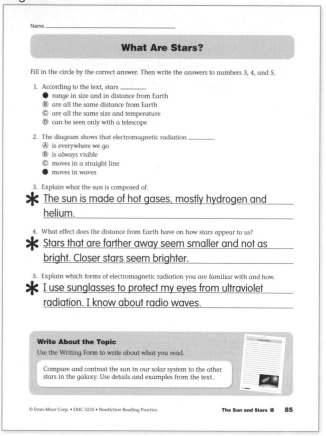

© Evan-Moor Corp. • EMC 3235 • Nonfiction Reading Practice   The Sun and Stars ▪   85

Page 87

Name _____

Look at the Stars

Fill in the circle by the correct answer. Then write the answers to numbers 3, 4, and 5.

1. The brightness of a star can indicate _____.
   - Ⓐ an entire galaxy
   - ⬤ a star's age
   - Ⓒ which telescope is required
   - Ⓓ a star's name

2. The sun appears bigger and brighter than other stars partly because it's _____.
   - Ⓐ farthest from Earth
   - Ⓑ near our solar system
   - Ⓒ yellow
   - ⬤ closest to Earth

3. Why do you think it's important for astronomers to study stars?

✳ It is important for us to know what our surroundings are. The sun is a star, and it affects life on Earth.

4. What inferences could you make about a small red star in the sky? Explain why.

✳ It is far from Earth. It's a cool star, because red stars are cooler. Interstellar matter could be there.

5. Did the photo help you understand the text better? Explain why or why not.

✳ Yes, I know what a telescope is, but I couldn't imagine one in orbit. I can see why it gets images others can't.

Write About the Topic

Use the Writing Form to write about what you read.

Explain how a scientist could use a star's appearance to learn more about stars and galaxies. Use details and examples.

© Evan-Moor Corp. • EMC 3235 • Nonfiction Reading Practice   The Sun and Stars ▪▪   87

Page 89

Name _____

Stars and Us

Fill in the circle by the correct answer. Then write the answers to numbers 3, 4, and 5.

1. A star's appearance can _____.
   - ⬤ indicate its age
   - Ⓑ indicate who discovered it
   - Ⓒ reveal its name
   - Ⓓ give clues about the telescope

2. Hubble depends on _____ to obtain clear deep-space images.
   - Ⓐ light in Earth's atmosphere
   - ⬤ light released from interstellar objects
   - Ⓒ Proxima Centauri and Barnard's Star
   - Ⓓ darkness emanating from Earth's surface

3. Would you rather study a Hubble image than one from another telescope? Why or why not?

✳ Hubble's images are clearer. They see deeper in space and show more detail because less light interferes.

4. Explain why stars differ in appearance.

✳ Stars change over time. Young stars glow red. Older stars look yellow, white, or blue.

5. If you could invent one tool to study stars, what would it be, and what would it do?

✳ I'd invent a super-fast ship that could withstand a star's heat so we could travel light-years to see it up close.

Write About the Topic

Use the Writing Form to write about what you read.

Is it important for astronomers to study stars? Write an argument for why or why not. Use details from the text.

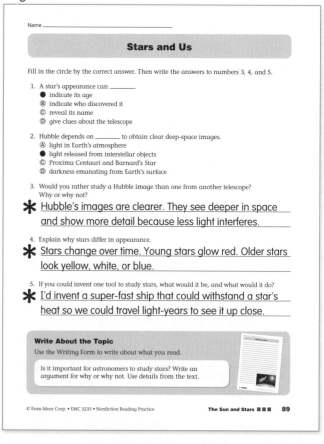

© Evan-Moor Corp. • EMC 3235 • Nonfiction Reading Practice   The Sun and Stars ▪▪▪   89

Page 95

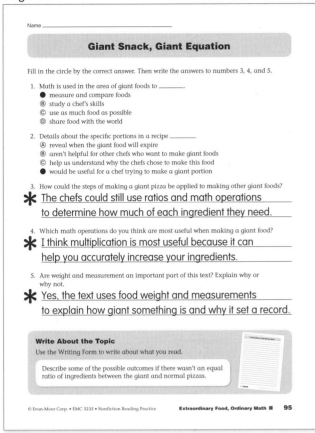

Name _____

Giant Snack, Giant Equation

Fill in the circle by the correct answer. Then write the answers to numbers 3, 4, and 5.

1. Math is used in the area of giant foods to _____.
   - ● measure and compare foods
   - Ⓑ study a chef's skills
   - Ⓒ use as much food as possible
   - Ⓓ share food with the world

2. Details about the specific portions in a recipe _____.
   - Ⓐ reveal when the giant food will expire
   - Ⓑ aren't helpful for other chefs who want to make giant foods
   - Ⓒ help us understand why the chefs chose to make this food
   - ● would be useful for a chef trying to make a giant portion

3. How could the steps of making a giant pizza be applied to making other giant foods?
   ✳ The chefs could still use ratios and math operations to determine how much of each ingredient they need.

4. Which math operations do you think are most useful when making a giant food?
   ✳ I think multiplication is most useful because it can help you accurately increase your ingredients.

5. Are weight and measurement an important part of this text? Explain why or why not.
   ✳ Yes, the text uses food weight and measurements to explain how giant something is and why it set a record.

Write About the Topic

Use the Writing Form to write about what you read.

Describe some of the possible outcomes if there wasn't an equal ratio of ingredients between the giant and normal pizzas.

© Evan-Moor Corp. • EMC 3235 • Nonfiction Reading Practice   **Extraordinary Food, Ordinary Math** ■   95

Page 97

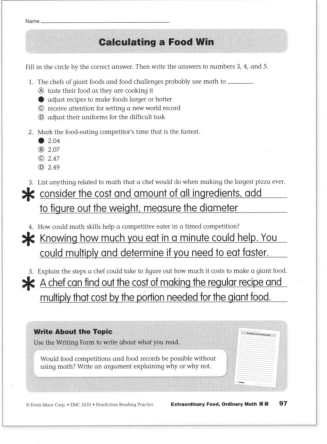

Name _____

Calculating a Food Win

Fill in the circle by the correct answer. Then write the answers to numbers 3, 4, and 5.

1. The chefs of giant foods and food challenges probably use math to _____.
   - Ⓐ taste their food as they are cooking it
   - ● adjust recipes to make foods larger or hotter
   - Ⓒ receive attention for setting a new world record
   - Ⓓ adjust their uniforms for the difficult task

2. Mark the food-eating competitor's time that is the fastest.
   - ● 2.04
   - Ⓑ 2.07
   - Ⓒ 2.47
   - Ⓓ 2.49

3. List anything related to math that a chef would do when making the largest pizza ever.
   ✳ consider the cost and amount of all ingredients, add to figure out the weight, measure the diameter

4. How could math skills help a competitive eater in a timed competition?
   ✳ Knowing how much you eat in a minute could help. You could multiply and determine if you need to eat faster.

5. Explain the steps a chef could take to figure out how much it costs to make a giant food.
   ✳ A chef can find out the cost of making the regular recipe and multiply that cost by the portion needed for the giant food.

Write About the Topic

Use the Writing Form to write about what you read.

Would food competitions and food records be possible without using math? Write an argument explaining why or why not.

© Evan-Moor Corp. • EMC 3235 • Nonfiction Reading Practice   **Extraordinary Food, Ordinary Math** ■ ■   97

Page 99

Name _____

Math Is a Chef's Friend

Fill in the circle by the correct answer. Then write the answers to numbers 3, 4, and 5.

1. Math is important in the area of giant foods because _____.
   - Ⓐ people enjoy using a lot of ingredients
   - Ⓑ the flavors of giant foods can be measured
   - ● it is used to measure and compare ratios of ingredients
   - Ⓓ it helps determine which ingredients are needed

2. Math is helpful in adjusting recipes because _____.
   - Ⓐ there are so many ingredients in all recipes
   - Ⓑ most people don't use recipes or measurements
   - Ⓒ it's not necessary to use accurate ingredients in most recipes
   - ● recipes have measurements that can be multiplied

3. Explain why ratios are important when chefs adjust recipes or make giant foods.
   ✳ The ratio of ingredients affects the result. Ratios must be the same for the giant size to taste like the regular size.

4. Could you apply the information in the text if you were trying to make a smaller version of a food? Explain why or why not.
   ✳ Yes. When you make a food bigger, you multiply the ingredients. When you make it smaller, you divide.

5. Do you agree with the title "Math Is a Chef's Friend"? Explain your answer.
   ✳ Yes, I agree that chefs rely on math to help them make good food, especially if they work in a busy restaurant.

Write About the Topic

Use the Writing Form to write about what you read.

Think of a food you can make. Explain the steps and the math operations you would use to make it for one hundred people.

© Evan-Moor Corp. • EMC 3235 • Nonfiction Reading Practice   **Extraordinary Food, Ordinary Math** ■ ■ ■   99

Page 105

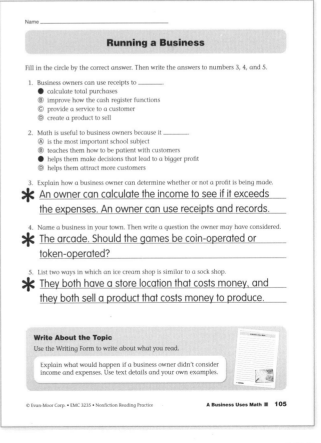

Name _____

Running a Business

Fill in the circle by the correct answer. Then write the answers to numbers 3, 4, and 5.

1. Business owners can use receipts to _____.
   - ● calculate total purchases
   - Ⓑ improve how the cash register functions
   - Ⓒ provide a service to a customer
   - Ⓓ create a product to sell

2. Math is useful to business owners because it _____.
   - Ⓐ is the most important school subject
   - Ⓑ teaches them how to be patient with customers
   - ● helps them make decisions that lead to a bigger profit
   - Ⓓ helps them attract more customers

3. Explain how a business owner can determine whether or not a profit is being made.
   ✳ An owner can calculate the income to see if it exceeds the expenses. An owner can use receipts and records.

4. Name a business in your town. Then write a question the owner may have considered.
   ✳ The arcade. Should the games be coin-operated or token-operated?

5. List two ways in which an ice cream shop is similar to a sock shop.
   ✳ They both have a store location that costs money, and they both sell a product that costs money to produce.

Write About the Topic

Use the Writing Form to write about what you read.

Explain what would happen if a business owner didn't consider income and expenses. Use text details and your own examples.

© Evan-Moor Corp. • EMC 3235 • Nonfiction Reading Practice   **A Business Uses Math** ■   105

Page 107

Name _____

All Businesses Use Math

Fill in the circle by the correct answer. Then write the answers to numbers 3, 4, and 5.

1. Which is a similarity between a restaurant and a bookstore?
   - Ⓐ Its main expense has an expiration date.
   - Ⓑ The business uses equipment to make its products.
   - Ⓒ Customers purchase a product they can use for years.
   - ● Customers pay to receive a product.

2. Business owners could _____ if they notice that their expenses exceed their income.
   - Ⓐ change their purpose
   - ● cut expenses by using cheaper materials
   - Ⓒ hire more staff and give them a raise in pay
   - Ⓓ change the store's hours to a time that's less busy

3. Describe some math operations a business owner could use to calculate a day's income.

   ✱ An owner can add receipt totals, then multiply the staff's hourly pay for the day, subtracting it from the income.

4. Why would owners choose to keep a business open for fewer hours?

   ✱ They have to pay employees' salaries for all the hours. The cost of being open could be high.

5. Why are profits significant for a business?

   ✱ A business needs to make money to pay its expenses. An owner makes money when income exceeds costs.

Write About the Topic

Use the Writing Form to write about what you read.

Do math and money affect every decision a business owner makes? Write an argument for why or why not. Use text details.

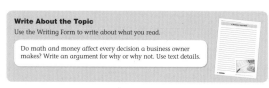

© Evan-Moor Corp. • EMC 3235 • Nonfiction Reading Practice   **A Business Uses Math** ■■ 107

Page 109

Name _____

Making a Profit

Fill in the circle by the correct answer. Then write the answers to numbers 3, 4, and 5.

1. Business owners who calculate their business's average weekly income _____.
   - Ⓐ must have a successful business
   - Ⓑ probably make business decisions without considering records
   - Ⓒ cannot estimate how much their expenses will be per week
   - ● can estimate how much money the business makes in a year

2. A business is not profitable if _____.
   - Ⓐ the expenses are covered by the income
   - Ⓑ the owner has too few staff members
   - ● its expenses exceed its income
   - Ⓓ its income exceeds its expenses

3. Explain how math plays a role in a business owner's decision making.

   ✱ Math is used to determine if an expense is worth it or if a profit is being made; it helps to balance income and cost.

4. Why is time an important consideration for business owners?

   ✱ Time affects an owner's ability to make money and influences decisions about what hours to stay open.

5. Could a business owner be successful without financial records? Explain your answer.

   ✱ You need a record of income and expenses. These show how much money goes in and out of the business.

Write About the Topic

Use the Writing Form to write about what you read.

Describe an idea for your own business. Tell what its purpose is and other details. Explain how you'd use math to make a profit.

© Evan-Moor Corp. • EMC 3235 • Nonfiction Reading Practice   **A Business Uses Math** ■■■ 109

Page 115

Name _____

Math and Video Games

Fill in the circle by the correct answer. Then write the answers to numbers 3, 4, and 5.

1. Video game developers use variables _____.
   - ● to receive data
   - Ⓑ to operate a game controller
   - Ⓒ to hold values on a coordinate plane
   - Ⓓ to apply geometry

2. The main idea of this text is that math _____.
   - Ⓐ has nothing to do with art in video games
   - Ⓑ doesn't affect video game players
   - Ⓒ is helpful but not necessary in creating a video game
   - ● is essential in creating a video game

3. Describe a video game you are familiar with and how geometry is used.

   ✱ I play Mario Kart, and it uses geometry to create the track and the obstacles on the track.

4. How does physics affect your game play?

   ✱ Physics makes the game characters and actions move and behave like the real world.

5. Based on the text, what inference can you make about video game developers?

   ✱ Video game developers have to be excellent at math and understand how it affects game play.

Write About the Topic

Use the Writing Form to write about what you read.

Compare and contrast how you use math skills at school with how a game developer uses math skills.

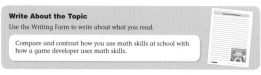

© Evan-Moor Corp. • EMC 3235 • Nonfiction Reading Practice   **Video Game Development** ■ 115

Page 117

Name _____

Math at Play

Fill in the circle by the correct answer. Then write the answers to numbers 3, 4, and 5.

1. Video game developers use variables _____.
   - Ⓐ to make a coordinate plane
   - Ⓑ to follow the laws of physics
   - ● instead of trying to anticipate every possibility
   - Ⓓ to interact with objects in a game

2. We see physics as applied math in the real world when we _____.
   - Ⓐ see obstacles in a game
   - ● run into something
   - Ⓒ see how colorful a game environment is
   - Ⓓ choose a character to play the game as or with

3. Describe a video game you are familiar with and how geometry is used.

   ✱ I play Legend of Zelda, and geometry is used to create obstacles that Link has to overcome.

4. What is the main idea of this text?

   ✱ Math is used to create almost everything in video games, and players don't even realize how much math is used.

5. Could a video game be created without using math? Explain why or why not.

   ✱ No, because nothing in the game would make sense. The scores, sizes, and times would be wrong.

Write About the Topic

Use the Writing Form to write about what you read.

Describe what a video game would be like if the developer used inaccurate math. Use your own examples and text details.

© Evan-Moor Corp. • EMC 3235 • Nonfiction Reading Practice   **Video Game Development** ■■ 117

✳ These answers will vary. Examples given.

Page 119

Name _____

The Game Developer's Toolkit

Fill in the circle by the correct answer. Then write the answers to numbers 3, 4, and 5.

1. Developers use variables _____.
   - Ⓐ to establish directives
   - ● to execute a function
   - Ⓒ to hard-code every possibility
   - Ⓓ to hold values

2. A game developer can use geometry to _____.
   - Ⓐ plot a character's location on a coordinate plane
   - Ⓑ create a vector
   - ● create obstacles in the game
   - Ⓓ define a variable

3. What would happen if a video game did not use vectors?
   ✳ The game would not know where or at what speed to move because it would not have the values it needs.

4. In your own words, explain pathfinding.
   ✳ Pathfinding is when the computer finds the shortest route between two points.

5. Explain why physics is important in a video game.
   ✳ Without physics, my character would walk through walls or never stop falling after a jump. Physics makes games more realistic.

Write About the Topic
Use the Writing Form to write about what you read.

Explain how a game developer uses math to create a video game. Use details from the text.

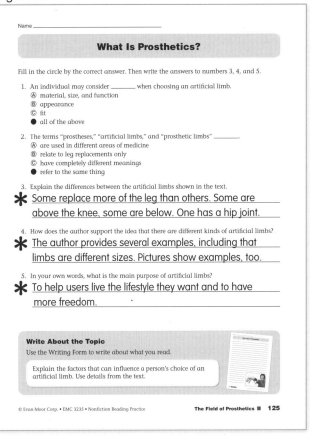

Page 125

Name _____

What Is Prosthetics?

Fill in the circle by the correct answer. Then write the answers to numbers 3, 4, and 5.

1. An individual may consider _____ when choosing an artificial limb.
   - Ⓐ material, size, and function
   - Ⓑ appearance
   - Ⓒ fit
   - ● all of the above

2. The terms "prostheses," "artificial limbs," and "prosthetic limbs" _____.
   - Ⓐ are used in different areas of medicine
   - Ⓑ relate to leg replacements only
   - Ⓒ have completely different meanings
   - ● refer to the same thing

3. Explain the differences between the artificial limbs shown in the text.
   ✳ Some replace more of the leg than others. Some are above the knee, some are below. One has a hip joint.

4. How does the author support the idea that there are different kinds of artificial limbs?
   ✳ The author provides several examples, including that limbs are different sizes. Pictures show examples, too.

5. In your own words, what is the main purpose of artificial limbs?
   ✳ To help users live the lifestyle they want and to have more freedom.

Write About the Topic
Use the Writing Form to write about what you read.

Explain the factors that can influence a person's choice of an artificial limb. Use details from the text.

Page 127

Name _____

Prosthetics Innovation

Fill in the circle by the correct answer. Then write the answers to numbers 3, 4, and 5.

1. What is the main idea of this text?
   - Ⓐ Artistic creativity has improved the quality of artificial limbs.
   - ● Technology has improved the quality of artificial limbs over time.
   - Ⓒ The earliest uses of prosthetics were better than today's.
   - Ⓓ The oldest prosthetic device is 3,000 years old.

2. Why were the earliest artificial limbs more simple?
   - ● Technology wasn't as advanced back then.
   - Ⓑ Technology was more advanced back then.
   - Ⓒ They didn't have any of the same materials we have now.
   - Ⓓ People didn't need artificial limbs back then.

3. What is one possible challenge knights using an iron artificial limb had? Why?
   ✳ Movement and flexibility would have been a challenge. Iron does not bend.

4. Which areas of prosthetics technology have seen improvement over the years?
   ✳ Prosthetics attach to the body better now, and prosthetics with hinges allow them to bend.

5. Are today's prosthetic limbs necessarily better than those of the past? Why or why not?
   ✳ They are probably better, because the materials look more natural and the limbs have better movement.

Write About the Topic
Use the Writing Form to write about what you read.

Compare and contrast how prosthetics was in its early days with how it is now. Use details from the text.

Page 129

Name _____

Prosthetics: Past and Present

Fill in the circle by the correct answer. Then write the answers to numbers 3, 4, and 5.

1. Why did doctors in the 1500s most likely seek to change prosthetics?
   - Ⓐ They wanted to make prosthetics a more popular field of medicine.
   - ● They thought adding joints could improve the user's movement.
   - Ⓒ Prosthetics technology at that time was extremely advanced.
   - Ⓓ Artificial limbs didn't exist during the Middle Ages.

2. The archaeological discovery in Egypt was significant because it showed that _____.
   - Ⓐ ancient civilizations had knights
   - Ⓑ ancient civilizations had computer technology
   - ● prosthetics existed in ancient civilizations
   - Ⓓ prosthetics didn't exist thousands of years ago

3. How does the photo support the main idea of the text?
   ✳ The athlete uses a prosthetic limb, which supports the idea that people need durable prosthetic options now.

4. How have people's expectations of prosthetics changed over time?
   ✳ People expect more durable, flexible prosthetics now. People expect high-functioning prosthetics.

5. What does the author mean by stating that early prosthetic designs still apply today?
   ✳ It means that even though a lot has changed and we have more technology now, we still use the early ideas.

Write About the Topic
Use the Writing Form to write about what you read.

Should more advancements in prosthetics be made if current prosthetics already work? Write an argument for why or why not.

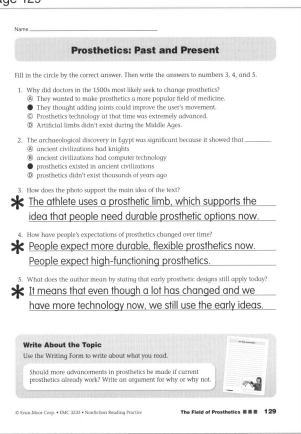

Page 135

Name _____

What Engineers Do

Fill in the circle by the correct answer. Then write the answers to numbers 3, 4, and 5.

1. Air travel would _____ without engineers.
   - Ⓐ continue
   - Ⓑ be safer
   - ● be impossible
   - Ⓓ be possible

2. A civil engineer probably considers _____ when designing a highway.
   - Ⓐ the amount of sunlight
   - ● the weight of vehicles
   - Ⓒ how much water is used daily
   - Ⓓ the number of families per U.S. state

3. List two things you've done that were probably possible because of engineering.

   ✳ I have ridden on a roller coaster, and I have been in a vehicle on a highway many times.

4. Why do you think engineers are needed in so many different fields and specialties?

   ✳ There are many areas in which we need safe, reliable structures and technology.

5. How does the author support the idea that engineering is competitive?

   ✳ The author gives an example of how engineers try to improve past designs, such as cars.

Write About the Topic

Use the Writing Form to write about what you read.

Explain how the world would be different without engineers. Use details from the text and your own examples.

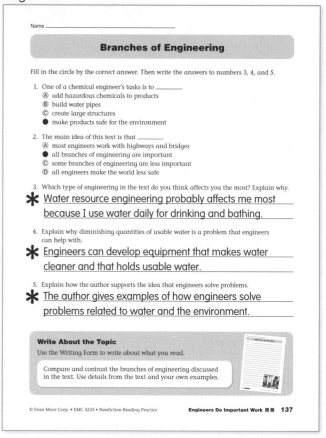

Page 137

Name _____

Branches of Engineering

Fill in the circle by the correct answer. Then write the answers to numbers 3, 4, and 5.

1. One of a chemical engineer's tasks is to _____.
   - Ⓐ add hazardous chemicals to products
   - Ⓑ build water pipes
   - Ⓒ create large structures
   - ● make products safe for the environment

2. The main idea of this text is that _____.
   - Ⓐ most engineers work with highways and bridges
   - ● all branches of engineering are important
   - Ⓒ some branches of engineering are less important
   - Ⓓ all engineers make the world less safe

3. Which type of engineering in the text do you think affects you the most? Explain why.

   ✳ Water resource engineering probably affects me most because I use water daily for drinking and bathing.

4. Explain why diminishing quantities of usable water is a problem that engineers can help with.

   ✳ Engineers can develop equipment that makes water cleaner and that holds usable water.

5. Explain how the author supports the idea that engineers solve problems.

   ✳ The author gives examples of how engineers solve problems related to water and the environment.

Write About the Topic

Use the Writing Form to write about what you read.

Compare and contrast the branches of engineering discussed in the text. Use details from the text and your own examples.

Page 139

Name _____

Engineers Start with a Concept

Fill in the circle by the correct answer. Then write the answers to numbers 3, 4, and 5.

1. What does the author mean by stating "an engineer made it real"?
   - Ⓐ Engineers are hired by people who need ideas.
   - Ⓑ Engineers are the people who usually have good ideas.
   - Ⓒ Ideas are real, and objects are not real.
   - ● A concept is just an idea until someone figures out how to build it.

2. Having scientific knowledge helps an engineer to _____.
   - Ⓐ determine whether or not to follow the engineering process
   - Ⓑ learn more about theme parks
   - ● create a design that could work in its environment
   - Ⓓ learn more about rules at hospitals

3. List some things that you use that were probably designed by an engineer.

   ✳ my cellphone, my computer, my remote control car, my PE shoes, the bridge near my house

4. Why is it important for engineers to use a process?

   ✳ The process helps the engineers create a safer thing that will actually work.

5. If the final product failed the testing stage, what do you think an engineer would do?

   ✳ The engineer would probably make changes to the design to see if all the hard work could be saved.

Write About the Topic

Use the Writing Form to write about what you read.

Think of something created by an engineer. Explain how an engineer used the process to create it and what considerations the engineer probably made. Use text details.

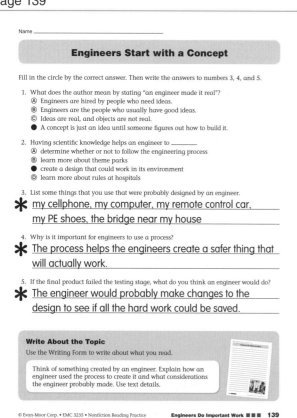

Page 145

Name _____

An Invention We Depend On

Fill in the circle by the correct answer. Then write the answers to numbers 3, 4, and 5.

1. Joseph Swan was probably _____.
   - Ⓐ a candle maker
   - Ⓑ a customer
   - Ⓒ an architect
   - ● a scientist

2. Why does the author state that light bulbs were a "luxury"?
   - ● They weren't common.
   - Ⓑ They were viewed similarly to how they're viewed today.
   - Ⓒ They didn't change the things that people were able to do.
   - Ⓓ Everyone had them in their homes during the 1800s.

3. Write one of the main ideas of the text.

   ✳ A lot of people worked for many years to create the light bulb. The light bulb has changed the way people live.

4. Why was it significant that lights could be placed in new places such as elevators?

   ✳ People could use elevators at night. People could extend their hours for work and play because of light bulbs.

5. Why do you think scientists spent so much time creating a constant stream of light?

   ✳ A long stream of dependable light allows people to work and read and do other activities.

Write About the Topic

Use the Writing Form to write about what you read.

Who should receive credit for the invention of the light bulbs we use today? Write an argument using details from the text.

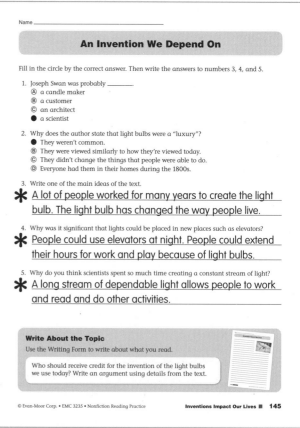

Page 147

Name _____

Creative Inventions

Fill in the circle by the correct answer. Then write the answers to numbers 3, 4, and 5.

1. The main idea of the text is that _____.
   - Ⓐ people invent things for no specific reason
   - ● inventions make our lives easier and better
   - Ⓒ inventions are usually silly and fun
   - Ⓓ all inventions have practical uses

2. People invent things _____.
   - ● for many different purposes
   - Ⓑ mainly for attention
   - Ⓒ mostly for comfort
   - Ⓓ for work

3. Is an invention more, less, or equally valuable if created by accident? Explain why.

   ✳ An invention can be valuable even if created by accident. Some silly inventions are created on purpose.

4. What does the author mean by stating that some inventions allowed further progress?

   ✳ The author uses the computer as an example. The first computer was good, but its technology kept improving.

5. Which of the "wacky" inventions did you find most surprising, and why?

   ✳ The finger fork is funny because I can't imagine using a fork that way. It's not like it's hard to just hold a fork!

Write About the Topic

Use the Writing Form to write about what you read.

Describe what the world would be like if people didn't invent new things. Use your own examples and details from the text.

Page 149

Name _____

Technology and Inventions

Fill in the circle by the correct answer. Then write the answers to numbers 3, 4, and 5.

1. A search-and-rescue drone would likely be used to _____.
   - Ⓐ protect people from natural disasters
   - Ⓑ help with food preparation
   - ● go to locations that are too dangerous for people
   - Ⓓ make people feel comfortable in their homes

2. Why does the author include the questions in the table?
   - Ⓐ These are the only important questions about society.
   - Ⓑ The answers to all the questions can be found in the text.
   - Ⓒ The author wants readers to memorize the answers to the questions.
   - ● The questions encourage readers to think about different aspects of society.

3. How does the author support the idea that technology reveals information about society?

   ✳ The author provides examples of the types of questions we can answer by looking at technology.

4. Write one of the main ideas from the text.

   ✳ Technology can reveal information about the society that uses it.

5. People have invented things for centuries. What does this say about us?

   ✳ It means that people have a need to improve their lives and to make progress.

Write About the Topic

Use the Writing Form to write about what you read.

What can you infer about a community from looking at its technology? Use a specific community as an example.

Page 155

Name _____

Augusta Savage's Work

Fill in the circle by the correct answer. Then write the answers to numbers 3, 4, and 5.

1. Augusta showed determination by _____.
   - Ⓐ sculpting with her thirteen siblings
   - Ⓑ using red clay to create sculptures
   - ● finding a way to sculpt after not being able to get red clay
   - Ⓓ spending money on expensive sculpting materials

2. In the photo, Augusta appears as though she is probably _____.
   - ● content
   - Ⓑ confused
   - Ⓒ stressed out
   - Ⓓ bored

3. Do you think the county fair was an important event in Augusta's life? Why or why not?

   ✳ Yes, because she could sell her art, and she realized that she had talent because people bought her art.

4. Did Augusta respond appropriately to the selection committee's decision? Why or why not?

   ✳ Yes, because its decision was unfair. She tried to let everyone know it was unfair. Talent does not have a color.

5. Why do you think Augusta supported other African American artists?

   ✳ She was an African American artist who struggled with racism herself. She knew how hard she had to work.

Write About the Topic

Use the Writing Form to write about what you read.

Explain how Augusta showed determination in pursuing her interests despite obstacles. Use details from the text.

Page 157

Name _____

An Artist and Activist

Fill in the circle by the correct answer. Then write the answers to numbers 3, 4, and 5.

1. It was difficult for Augusta to develop her sculpting skills _____.
   - Ⓐ with red clay
   - Ⓑ at the Harlem Community Art Center
   - Ⓒ at the Savage Studio of Arts and Crafts
   - ● with little support from her father

2. Augusta was the director of the art center most likely because _____.
   - Ⓐ she had the least amount of experience with art
   - ● she was passionate about supporting other African American artists
   - Ⓒ nobody else believed in the cause of supporting other artists
   - Ⓓ free art instruction wouldn't provide a large income

3. Describe how Augusta responded to struggles in her life.

   ✳ She didn't let hardship stop her from doing what she wanted. She challenged things she didn't agree with.

4. How does the author support the idea that Augusta was an activist?

   ✳ The author describes how Augusta handled racism and gives examples of the work Augusta did to help others.

5. What do you admire or dislike about Augusta Savage? Explain why.

   ✳ I admire that Augusta kept sculpting even though she didn't have support in the beginning.

Write About the Topic

Use the Writing Form to write about what you read.

Describe three personality traits that you think Augusta had, and support these statements using text details.

✱ These answers will vary. Examples given.

Page 159

Name _____

Augusta Savage's Life

Fill in the circle by the correct answer. Then write the answers to numbers 3, 4, and 5.

1. Augusta was probably hopeful that contacting newspapers would _____.
   - ● encourage the selection committee to change its decision
   - Ⓑ make newspaper readers more interested in art
   - Ⓒ make the committee cancel the art program in France
   - Ⓓ encourage the selection committee to reject other applicants, too

2. Augusta's art and activism most likely _____.
   - Ⓐ caused her nephew to be embarrassed
   - Ⓑ allowed fewer African Americans to become artists
   - Ⓒ encouraged more writers to ask for busts of themselves
   - ● helped change perceptions of African Americans for the better

3. Explain why it was probably important for Augusta to make art accessible to all races.
   ✱ Augusta had little support for her own interest in art early on. She also experienced racism in her art studies.

4. Write one question you would ask Augusta if you could interview her today.
   ✱ Did you feel proud when you were asked to make the sculpture for the 1939 World's Fair?

5. Describe the sculpture *Gamin*. What feeling do you get from it?
   ✱ The sculpture is of a young boy who looks serious. I feel like he might be sad.

Write About the Topic
Use the Writing Form to write about what you read.

Explain how Augusta affected future generations with her work. Use details and examples to support your answer.

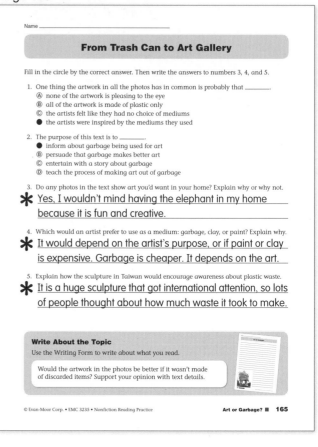

© Evan-Moor Corp. • EMC 3235 • Nonfiction Reading Practice   **Augusta Savage ■■■ 159**

Page 165

Name _____

From Trash Can to Art Gallery

Fill in the circle by the correct answer. Then write the answers to numbers 3, 4, and 5.

1. One thing the artwork in all the photos has in common is probably that _____.
   - Ⓐ none of the artwork is pleasing to the eye
   - Ⓑ all of the artwork is made of plastic only
   - Ⓒ the artists felt like they had no choice of mediums
   - ● the artists were inspired by the mediums they used

2. The purpose of this text is to _____.
   - ● inform about garbage being used for art
   - Ⓑ persuade that garbage makes better art
   - Ⓒ entertain with a story about garbage
   - Ⓓ teach the process of making art out of garbage

3. Do any photos in the text show art you'd want in your home? Explain why or why not.
   ✱ Yes, I wouldn't mind having the elephant in my home because it is fun and creative.

4. Which would an artist prefer to use as a medium: garbage, clay, or paint? Explain why.
   ✱ It would depend on the artist's purpose, or if paint or clay is expensive. Garbage is cheaper. It depends on the art.

5. Explain how the sculpture in Taiwan would encourage awareness about plastic waste.
   ✱ It is a huge sculpture that got international attention, so lots of people thought about how much waste it took to make.

Write About the Topic
Use the Writing Form to write about what you read.

Would the artwork in the photos be better if it wasn't made of discarded items? Support your opinion with text details.

© Evan-Moor Corp. • EMC 3235 • Nonfiction Reading Practice   **Art or Garbage? ■ 165**

Page 167

Name _____

Unique Art

Fill in the circle by the correct answer. Then write the answers to numbers 3, 4, and 5.

1. The author probably decided on the title "Unique Art" because _____.
   - Ⓐ using garbage reduces waste
   - Ⓑ garbage is the only unique medium
   - ● art created from garbage is usually one-of-a-kind
   - Ⓓ plastic bag art has to be unique

2. One reason that Peter Singer created *World of Litter* could have been to _____.
   - Ⓐ create art that also serves as water transportation
   - Ⓑ spend time cleaning plastic bottles
   - Ⓒ teach other people how to become artists
   - ● raise awareness about environmental waste

3. Write two questions the text raised for you but didn't answer.
   ✱ 1) Is plastic the main form of waste used in most art?
   2) Do the artists who use garbage sell their artwork?

4. Describe one image shown in the text that you liked or found interesting.
   ✱ I like the snowy landscape art because it really looks like snow. It's believable.

5. Explain in your own words the difference between artistic methods and art mediums.
   ✱ Methods are actions artists can take to transform materials. Mediums are the materials artists use.

Write About the Topic
Use the Writing Form to write about what you read.

Write a short essay persuading artists why they should use garbage in their art. Use your own examples and text details.

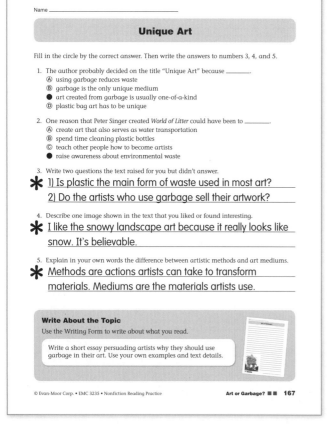

© Evan-Moor Corp. • EMC 3235 • Nonfiction Reading Practice   **Art or Garbage? ■■ 167**

Page 169

Name _____

One Person's Junk...

Fill in the circle by the correct answer. Then write the answers to numbers 3, 4, and 5.

1. The main idea of this text is that _____.
   - Ⓐ art that is avant-garde can't have a message
   - ● discarded items can be used to make art
   - Ⓒ only plastic bag art can be avant-garde
   - Ⓓ auto-destructive art always has a message

2. An example of auto-destructive art could be a _____.
   - ● rusty tricycle in a yard with plants growing around it
   - Ⓑ finger painting hanging on a clean wall
   - Ⓒ red jar filled with beans on a fresh white doily
   - Ⓓ framed drawing of a tree

3. Do you agree with the author about the popular saying quoted in the text? Why or why not?
   ✱ Yes, I agree. Someone threw away items, but an artist found a way to use them to make something to enjoy.

4. How did the author support the idea that garbage art is avant-garde?
   ✱ The author defined avant-garde as being unconventional. Using garbage for art is unconventional. The wreath shown is, too.

5. What does artwork with traditional mediums have in common with garbage artwork?
   ✱ Art with traditional mediums can also have an important message and be avant-garde.

Write About the Topic
Use the Writing Form to write about what you read.

Is all garbage art avant-garde or sharing an important message? Write an argument for why or why not.

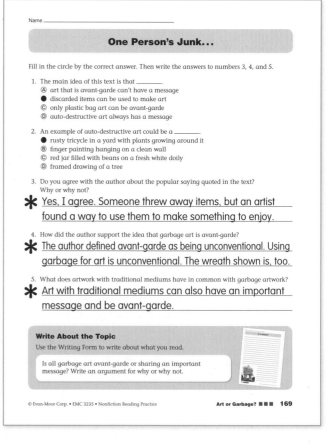

© Evan-Moor Corp. • EMC 3235 • Nonfiction Reading Practice   **Art or Garbage? ■■■ 169**

These answers will vary. Examples given.

Page 175

Name _____

Staying at an Ice Hotel

Fill in the circle by the correct answer. Then write the answers to numbers 3, 4, and 5.

1. One reason ice hotel visitors should wear a lot of layers is that _____.
   Ⓐ the ice hotel does not provide shelter
   ● temperatures can drop below zero
   Ⓒ they can stay in a warm room
   Ⓓ there are furs and animal skins on the beds

2. It would be most unlikely to find an ice hotel in _____.
   ● Australia
   Ⓑ Russia
   Ⓒ Switzerland
   Ⓓ Greenland

3. How does the Art Suite in the photo compare to a hotel room you've stayed in before?
   ✳ I haven't stayed in a room that had bear figures in it. I haven't seen a bed with thick fur blankets or ice blocks.

4. Explain the purpose of putting a mattress and sleeping bags on the beds.
   ✳ The purpose is probably to create a barrier between the icy bed and the body. It allows the person to feel warm.

5. Would you rather stay in a traditional hotel or an ice hotel? Explain why.
   ✳ I'd rather stay in a traditional one most of the time, but I'd like to try the ice hotel because it would be unique.

Write About the Topic
Use the Writing Form to write about what you read.

How are ice hotels similar to other hotels you know about? How are they different? Use details from the text.

© Evan-Moor Corp. • EMC 3235 • Nonfiction Reading Practice   Ice Hotels ■ 175

Page 177

Name _____

People Love Ice Hotels

Fill in the circle by the correct answer. Then write the answers to numbers 3, 4, and 5.

1. Ice hotels are similar to traditional hotels because they both usually _____.
   Ⓐ have snice in their buildings
   Ⓑ stay open for only a few months every year
   Ⓒ require multiple layers of clothing
   ● offer beds, food, and entertainment

2. Which detail supports the idea that ice hotels are beautiful?
   Ⓐ The rooms can get very cold.
   ● They are built by artists.
   Ⓒ There are food and drink vendors.
   Ⓓ One of them has an area of 60,000 square feet (5,500 square meters).

3. Could an ice hotel be successful without snice? Explain why or why not.
   ✳ Possibly, but not as successful. Snice is denser than snow, so it insulates better and prevents quicker melting.

4. Why would someone choose to host a large event at an ice hotel?
   ✳ Ice hotels are beautiful and majestic. They have large banquet halls. They are unique.

5. What can you infer about ice hotels from the fact that they attract so many guests?
   ✳ They are well liked. People enjoy staying there, and they think it's fun and comfortable.

Write About the Topic
Use the Writing Form to write about what you read.

Write a short essay persuading a friend that it would be safe and fun to stay at an ice hotel. Use details from the text.

© Evan-Moor Corp. • EMC 3235 • Nonfiction Reading Practice   Ice Hotels ■ ■ 177

Page 179

Name _____

Ice Hotel: A Modern Symbol

Fill in the circle by the correct answer. Then write the answers to numbers 3, 4, and 5.

1. The main idea of this text is that ice hotels symbolize _____.
   Ⓐ the values of the countries they are built in
   Ⓑ how travelers should behave
   ● an excellent modern traveling experience
   Ⓓ the strengths and weaknesses of hotels

2. The bold headings in the text indicate _____, according to the author.
   Ⓐ traits that people find only in ice hotels
   Ⓑ things that people are trying to avoid
   Ⓒ what Sweden, Canada, Finland, Norway, and Romania are known for
   ● things that modern travelers value

3. Ice hotels have become popular in a short time. What does this suggest about them?
   ✳ It suggests that ice hotels provide people with a good experience. It means people like them.

4. Is it significant that artists help build ice hotels? Explain why or why not.
   ✳ Yes, because it supports the idea that the hotels are innovative. A lot of thought goes into the hotel's look.

5. Do you think the author would stay in an ice hotel? Explain why or why not.
   ✳ I think the author would stay in an ice hotel because of the positive comments and facts in the text.

Write About the Topic
Use the Writing Form to write about what you read.

Is the author's claim that ice hotels symbolize what modern travelers value convincing? Use details from the text for support.

© Evan-Moor Corp. • EMC 3235 • Nonfiction Reading Practice   Ice Hotels ■ ■ ■ 179

© Evan-Moor Corp. • EMC 3235 • Nonfiction Reading Practice

199

Sample Lesson

Daily **6-Trait** **Writing** **GRADE 5**

DAY 1

Read the rule aloud. Explain that **to elaborate** means "to develop further or tell more about something." Then guide students through the activities.

- **Activity A:** Have students read both letters. Then say: *Pat's letter says the students used to have fun in the writer's club. Rula's letter says the club members used to have fun staying after school and thinking up stories to write. Which writer elaborated on the details more?* (Rula) Continue to go through the letters, comparing details. Then have students write their answers to the question.

- **Activity B (Convention):** Say: *Negative words are words such as* **no, not, never, nothing, nobody,** *and* **nowhere.** *Using two negatives in a sentence is called using a double negative. When you see double negatives, you should remove one, because you only need one.* Read sentence 1 aloud and ask: *What is the double negative?* ("don't live nowhere") *How could we change that sentence to make it correct?* ("The students don't live anywhere near..." or "The students live nowhere near...") Model using proofreading marks to correct the sentence. Repeat the process for the second sentence.

DAY 2

Read the rule aloud. Then guide students through the activities.

- **Activity A:** Read the essay aloud. Say: *This essay's ideas are too general. The lack of specific examples makes the paragraph boring.* Point out the word **things** and ask: *What are some specific things that a photograph can help you remember?* Use the students' answers to model filling in the first box. Have students complete the rest of the chart independently. Then review the answers.

- **Activity B (Convention):** Review the definition of double negatives. Then read aloud sentence 1 and say: *Never is a negative because it means "not ever." Couldn't is a negative because it is a contraction for* **could not.** *So, what is the double negative?* (**couldn't never**) Say: *There are two ways to fix this: "I could never give up my camera" or "I couldn't ever give up my camera."* Have students complete the activity independently.

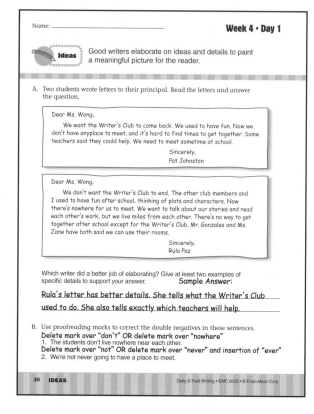

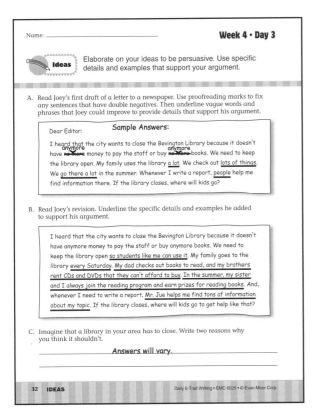

Name: _____   **Week 4 • Day 3**

Ideas   Elaborate on your ideas to be persuasive. Use specific details and examples that support your argument.

A. Read Joey's first draft of a letter to a newspaper. Use proofreading marks to fix any sentences that have double negatives. Then underline vague words and phrases that Joey could improve to provide details that support his argument.

Dear Editor: **Sample Answers:**

I heard that the city wants to close the Bevington Library because it doesn't have ~~no more~~ money to pay the staff or buy ~~no more~~ books. We need to keep the library open. My family uses the library <u>a lot</u>. We check out <u>lots of things</u>. We go there <u>a lot</u> in the summer. Whenever I write a report, <u>people help me</u> find information there. If the library closes, where will kids go?

B. Read Joey's revision. Underline the specific details and examples he added to support his argument.

I heard that the city wants to close the Bevington Library because it doesn't have anymore money to pay the staff or buy anymore books. We need to keep the library open <u>so students like me can use it. My family goes to the library every Saturday. My dad checks out books to read, and my brothers rent CDs and DVDs that they can't afford to buy. In the summer, my sister and I always join the reading program and earn prizes for reading books. And, whenever I need to write a report, Mr. Jue helps me find tons of information about my topic.</u> If the library closes, where will kids go to get help like that?

C. Imagine that a library in your area has to close. Write two reasons why you think it shouldn't.

_____ Answers will vary. _____
_____

32   IDEAS   Daily 6-Trait Writing • EMC 6025 • © Evan-Moor Corp.

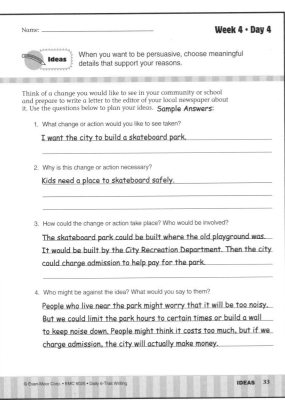

Name: _____   **Week 4 • Day 4**

Ideas   When you want to be persuasive, choose meaningful details that support your reasons.

Think of a change you would like to see in your community or school and prepare to write a letter to the editor of your local newspaper about it. Use the questions below to plan your ideas. **Sample Answers:**

1. What change or action would you like to see taken?
   <u>I want the city to build a skateboard park.</u>

2. Why is this change or action necessary?
   <u>Kids need a place to skateboard safely.</u>

3. How could the change or action take place? Who would be involved?
   <u>The skateboard park could be built where the old playground was. It would be built by the City Recreation Department. Then the city could charge admission to help pay for the park.</u>

4. Who might be against the idea? What would you say to them?
   <u>People who live near the park might worry that it will be too noisy. But we could limit the park hours to certain times or build a wall to keep noise down. People might think it costs too much, but if we charge admission, the city will actually make money.</u>

© Evan-Moor Corp. • EMC 6025 • Daily 6-Trait Writing   **IDEAS** 33

DAY 3

Read the rule aloud. Then guide students through the activities.

- **Activity A (Convention):** Read the letter aloud and have students correct the double negatives. Then say: *Joey wrote this letter because he wants to persuade other people that the library shouldn't be closed. He has given several reasons but hasn't elaborated on them very well.* Direct students to the sentence "My family uses the library a lot." Ask: *Is this sentence specific? Does it tell us exactly how often or when they use the library?* (no) Guide students through the rest of the paragraph, underlining similarly vague statements.

- **Activity B:** Read the paragraph aloud. Then call students' attention to the third sentence ("My family goes to...") and ask: *What did Joey change?* (the word **a lot** to **every Saturday**) Ask: *Why is this better?* (It's more specific and meaningful.) Have students complete the activity in pairs.

- **Activity C:** After students write their reasons, invite volunteers to share what they wrote.

DAY 4

Read the rule aloud. Then guide students through the activity.

- Say: *A letter to a newspaper editor is often written to persuade readers to do something.* Point out that letters to the editor are typically about issues related to neighborhood improvement, recreation, public transportation, the environment, or crime. Help students brainstorm specific topics.

- Use the sample answers on the reduced page to the left to model answering the questions. For question 4, point out that it's important to think of possible arguments against your position so you can address them.

DAY 5 *Writing Prompt*

- *Use your answers to the questions on Day 4 to write a letter to the editor about an important issue. Include specific details, examples, and reasons that elaborate on your opinion.*

- *Be sure to fix any double negatives in your letter.*

Ideas Good writers elaborate on ideas and details to paint a meaningful picture for the reader.

A. Two students wrote letters to their principal. Read the letters and answer the question.

Dear Ms. Wong,

We want the Writer's Club to come back. We used to have fun. Now we don't have anyplace to meet, and it's hard to find times to get together. Some teachers said they could help. We need to meet sometime at school.

Sincerely,
Pat Johnston

Dear Ms. Wong,

We don't want the Writer's Club to end. The other club members and I used to have fun after school, thinking of plots and characters. Now there's nowhere for us to meet. We want to talk about our stories and read each other's work, but we live miles from each other. There's no way to get together after school except for the Writer's Club. Mr. Gonzales and Ms. Zane have both said we can use their rooms.

Sincerely,
Rula Paz

Which writer did a better job of elaborating? Give at least two examples of specific details to support your answer.

_____

_____

B. Use proofreading marks to correct the double negatives in these sentences.

1. The students don't live nowhere near each other.

2. We're not never going to have a place to meet.

 **Ideas**

Look for ways to elaborate on your ideas by making your details and examples more specific.

A. Read this short essay. The words in bold are not very specific. How could the writer have elaborated more on her ideas? Use the chart below to write more specific examples the writer might have included instead.

> Photographs are a good way to help remember **things**. **Important events** in my life are shown through photos. Photos help me remember the **fun times** with my friends.

Too General	More Specific
things	
important events	
fun times	

B. Rewrite each sentence to fix the double negative.

1. I couldn't never give up my camera.

   _____

2. Stacey doesn't want nobody to take her picture.

   _____

3. There's not nothing better than taking pictures.

   _____

Ideas   Elaborate on your ideas to be persuasive. Use specific details and examples that support your argument.

A. Read Joey's first draft of a letter to a newspaper. Use proofreading marks to fix any sentences that have double negatives. Then underline vague words and phrases that Joey could improve to provide details that support his argument.

> Dear Editor:
>
> I heard that the city wants to close the Bevington Library because it doesn't have no more money to pay the staff or buy no more books. We need to keep the library open. My family uses the library a lot. We check out lots of things. We go there a lot in the summer. Whenever I write a report, people help me find information there. If the library closes, where will kids go?

B. Read Joey's revision. Underline the specific details and examples he added to support his argument.

> I heard that the city wants to close the Bevington Library because it doesn't have anymore money to pay the staff or buy anymore books. We need to keep the library open so students like me can use it. My family goes to the library every Saturday. My dad checks out books to read, and my brothers rent CDs and DVDs that they can't afford to buy. In the summer, my sister and I always join the reading program and earn prizes for reading books. And, whenever I need to write a report, Mr. Jue helps me find tons of information about my topic. If the library closes, where will kids go to get help like that?

C. Imagine that a library in your area has to close. Write two reasons why you think it shouldn't.

_____

_____

Name: _____

 **Ideas** When you want to be persuasive, choose meaningful details that support your reasons.

Think of a change you would like to see in your community or school and prepare to write a letter to the editor of your local newspaper about it. Use the questions below to plan your ideas.

1. What change or action would you like to see taken?

   _____

   _____

2. Why is this change or action necessary?

   _____

   _____

   _____

3. How could the change or action take place? Who would be involved?

   _____

   _____

   _____

   _____

4. Who might be against the idea? What would you say to them?

   _____

   _____

   _____

   _____

SKILL SHARPENERS

PreK–6

SHARPENERS

Connecting School & Home

"Colorful and fun! Skill Sharpeners has successfully engaged my very easily distracted son. I highly recommend it."

—Parent, Cambridge, Idaho

Grades PreK–6 *Skill Sharpeners: Reading* provides at-home practice that helps students master and retain skills. Each book in this dynamic series is the ideal resource for programs such as summer school, after school, remediation, school book fairs, and fundraising.

- Activities aligned with current standards
- Assessment pages in standardized-test format
- Full-color, charmingly illustrated, and kid-friendly

144 full-color pages. **www.evan-moor.com/ssh**

 The National Parenting Center, Seal of Approval Winner

 iParenting Media Awards Outstanding Product

Reading

Activity Book
Print

GRADE	EMC
PreK	4527
K	4528
1	4529
2	4530
3	4531
4	4532
5	4533
6	4534

Reading Literary Text

Grades 1–6 Builds strong literary analysis and comprehension skills. Each unit provides literary text in a variety of genres such as myth, folk tale, comedy, realistic fiction, and historical fiction, as well as supporting activities that are easy to scaffold, including close reading, vocabulary, comprehension, literary analysis, and writing.

Includes guided reading levels and correlations to current standards and TEKS for easy reference. 144 pages. Correlated to current standards. Federal funding sources: I, 21 **www.evan-moor.com/rlt**

*Grade 1 includes minibooks

Teacher's Edition
Print

Teacher's Edition
E-book

Student Book
5-Pack

Student Book

GRADE	EMC		GRADE	EMC		GRADE	EMC		GRADE	EMC
1	3211		1	3211i		1	6491		1	6481
2	3212		2	3212i		2	6492		2	6482
3	3213		3	3213i		3	6493		3	6483
4	3214		4	3214i		4	6494		4	6484
5	3215		5	3215i		5	6495		5	6485
6	3216		6	3216i		6	6496		6	6486

Downloadable home–school connection activities and projects extend learning at home